RESTORATION LOVE SONGS

RESTORATION
Love Songs

EDITED BY JOHN HADFIELD

With decorations by Rex Whistler

THE CUPID PRESS
1950

OF THIS BOOK six hundred and sixty copies have been printed in Great Britain for the Cupid Press, Preston, near Hitchin, in Hertfordshire. The text has been set in the Fell types and printed at the University Press, Oxford, on Arnold & Foster's mould-made paper. The collotypes from drawings by Rex Whistler have also been printed at the University Press, Oxford. The binding, in hand-marbled boards by Douglas Cockerell & Son, is by the Temple Press, Letchworth.

This is number 140

'THIS MORNING, before I was up,' wrote Samuel Pepys in his diary on January 30th, 1659/60, 'I fell a-singing of my song, "Great, good and just, &c.," and put myself thereby in mind that this was the fatal day, now ten years since, his Majesty died.' Meanwhile clerks and apprentices, setting about their day's work, were quoting lewd doggerels about the Grandees of the Rump. London was restive and ill at ease. From lip to lip was passed the significant couplet:

> 'Tis hoped before the month of June
> The birds will sing another tune.

The hope was vouchsafed. On May 29th of that same year Charles the Second entered London, 'with a triumph of above twenty thousand horse and foot, brandishing their swords and shouting with inexpressible joy; the ways strewed with flowers, the bells ringing, the streets hung with tapestry, fountains running with wine'. Not only the birds, but all England burst into a new tune.

Historians are still divided in assessing the political consequences of the Restoration. Whatever may be their ultimate verdict, one thing is certain: the return of the Black Boy meant a restoration of wit, a resurgence of gaiety and song. The philistine sobriety of the Commonwealth had lain uneasily on the spirits of Stuart England. When he heard of the Restoration Sir Thomas Urquhart is said to have died of laughing. That was an apt, if over-emphatic, comment on the change which now spread across the face of his country.

Just as moralists have painted the Black Boy even darker than his raven locks, so sentimentalists have invested with an unreal glamour the gallantries of his Court. There was much that was merely bestial in the frolics of the town. Rochester was painting his own picture when he wrote (*if* he wrote):

> Room, room for a Blade of the Town,
> That takes delight in roaring,
> And daily rambles up and down
> And at night in the street lies snoaring.
> That for the noble name of Spark
> Dares his companions rally;
> Commits an outrage in the dark,
> Then slinks into an alley.

When considering the grosser immoralities of the Rakes, however, it is wise to place them in their historic setting. Restoration England retained many of the crude features of the Middle Ages. Duels, riots, and brawls were a commonplace of city life. Cock-fighting and bull-baiting were fashionable sports. The most respectable of men—lawyers, clergy, University dons—were often carried home incapably drunk. Disease was rampant. There was no sanitation. In the nine years whose daily occurrences Pepys recorded with intimate detail he only once mentioned having a bath. It is hardly to be expected that tenderness or delicacy of sentiment would thrive in such a state of society.

The group of Wits which included Sir Charles Sedley and Charles Sackville, Lord Buckhurst (later the Earl of Dorset), was chiefly responsible for setting the tone of fashionable morality and social behaviour. Professor de Sola Pinto, in his biography of Sedley, compares them with the generation which often follows a great war. Reacting against the solemn didacticism of the Commonwealth, they turned to the sensuous pleasures of a pagan philosophy.

> Let us enjoy the joys we know
>   Of musick, wine and love.
> We're sure of what we find below,
>   Uncertain what 's above.

Many of their excesses and escapades—such as the appearance of Sedley, Buckhurst, and Sir Thomas Ogle stark naked on the balcony of the Cock

Tavern, where Sedley delivered a blasphemous mock sermon to a crowd of over a thousand people—were the equivalent of undergraduate 'rags' in our own time. A few of the Wits, like Rochester in the next generation, pursued their mad course until they were overtaken by disease and remorse. It is significant, however, that, of the trio who enraged the Puritans by their unseemly pranks at the Cock Tavern, one, Sir Thomas Ogle, became a sober Governor of Chelsea College, another, Buckhurst, was soon happily married, and Sedley became a responsible Member of Parliament. All three grew old gracefully and lived into the eighteenth century. Etherege was the only notable figure amongst the Wits who continued his Rake's progress to the end.

If we regard the Court poets of the Restoration as high-spirited undergraduates, reacting against an older generation, and living in a world where cruelty, uncleanness, and the grosser appetites were taken for granted, the sensuality and inconstancy of their sentiments may be understood, if not forgiven. And what they lacked in decorum and constancy was certainly made up in ardour and wit.

The following selection of love lyrics, though guided first by criteria of poetic merit, does in fact illustrate a transition, through fifty-four years, from the passionate utterance of such cavalier poets as Carew, Lovelace, and Suckling to the rational scepticism of the Augustans.

The 'poor, suff'ring heart' of Dryden's song was no mere image of the mind. I think many readers who know Dryden best in his longer periods will be surprised at the depth of feeling revealed in some of his songs. As Mr. Quennell has said, 'their texture sometimes recalls a brocaded fabric, heavily ornamented and yet supple to the touch'. There is, however, something more than poetic mastery in such songs as No. 8, 'Secret Love', and No. 12, with its final superb, double-edged couplet:

> Time and Death shall depart, and say, in flying,
> Love has found out a way to live by dying.

Etheregе is, of course, the inconstant lover *in excelsis*, but even he, for all his scepticism, has an underlying tenderness of feeling:

> Cloris, at worst you'll in the end
> But change your lover for a friend.

Sedley, perhaps, never went quite out of his emotional depth, but Mr. Quennell's condemnation of him as a 'singularly vapid poetaster' is surely unjust. I confess to finding a real, if autumnal, feeling in Songs 15 and 17, especially when it is realized that the young Ann Ayscough to whom Song 17 is addressed, and to whom Sedley was unquestionably devoted, was destined to become his wife in every sense except that of law.

Dorset is perhaps the most engaging personality of them all. His levity was counterbalanced by his tenderness, his sensuality by his kindness. 'My Lord Dorset might do anything,' said Rochester, 'yet was never to blame.' No song of the period so confidently declares the world well lost for love as No. 24. How agreeable, at a time when men worship the Welfare State, is the bold statement that

> My love is full of noble pride,
> And never will submit
> To let that fop Discretion ride
> In triumph over Wit.

I take the year 1672 to be the high noon of the Restoration—or (should I say?) the midnight of the Rakes. This was the year which saw the publication of Kemp's *Collection of Poems*—a major source-book of the English lyric—*Covent Garden Drollery*, Robert Veal's *New Court-Songs*, and the second part of *Westminster Drollery*. In the following year appeared that interesting and largely unexplored miscellany called by the first line of Dorset's 'Methinks the Poor Town...'.

After this date the fever of the love lyric gradually declined. There were, of course, exceptions, such as the heart-cries of that mysterious jilt,

'Ephelia', and the plunging passions of the only poet amongst them all to approach the stature of Dryden—John Wilmot, Earl of Rochester. For all his fantastic irreverence, one can yet imagine Rochester, spent with excesses, echoing on his death-bed those lines of Vaughan:

> I played with fire, did counsell spurn,
>   Made life my common stake;
> But never thought that fire would burn,
>   Or that a soul could ake.

For the rest, the mainstream of the lyrical impulse was gradually diverted into a variety of rivulets. Some flowed into obscurity, like the exquisite metaphysical conceits of Richard Leigh or the intellectual antitheses of Philip Ayres—both of whom are restored in this collection to a position worthier of their merits. Matthew Coppinger and Thomas Heyrick are two other thoughtful writers in the minor key who had their own peculiar talent and charm, and deserve some reconsideration.

The light-hearted gallantry of Dorset, Sedley, and Etherege was fitfully sustained by John Sheffield, Duke of Buckinghamshire, and George Granville, Lord Lansdowne, both of whom have been curiously neglected by anthologists. With the Glorious Revolution, however, wit and scepticism finally triumphed over ardours and endurances. To

John Oldmixon—a prose hack but an accomplished versifier—love was a game, a convention. William Walsh's cynicism is only surpassed by that of Congreve, of whom F. W. Bateson aptly wrote: 'It is no inconsiderable achievement to contemplate sex under the dry light of irony.' With Congreve we enter the Age of Reason, when even the transports of love savoured of that unfashionable attribute, Enthusiasm, and when Honest Merry Harry Carey, who was capable of so sweet a sentimentality as 'Sally in Our Alley', nevertheless sang:

> If she does not love you, make her;
> When she loves you, then—forsake her;
> 'Tis the modish way of wooing.

Yet, though the mode of wooing may seem to have changed, though the lyrical impulse was now fired by a new fashion, one element had remained constant through the years—the rule of song. I began this Introduction by quoting Samuel Pepys. He, as everyone knows, found his chief delight in song. At the accession of Charles the Second, the day after the King's proclamation 'against drinking, swearing and debauchery' was, with a charming irony, read to the ships' companies in the Fleet, the Admiral, Lord Sandwich, called for the lieutenant's cittern, and, with two candlesticks filled with money for cymbals, he and Samuel Pepys made 'barber's music, with which my Lord was well pleased'. This is but one of a thousand examples of the rule of song in Restoration England.

In every household, every tavern or ale-house, it was customary to gather in the evening to sing glees or catches. In 1678 a small-coal merchant, Thomas Britton, began to give concerts in a loft above his warehouse in Clerkenwell. There, every night for forty years, could be heard the finest music in London. On the walls of barbers' shops hung citterns and guitars—as one might find copies of the weekly magazines today. Almost everyone could play some musical instrument. A special pride was taken in mastering the various graces affected by the lutenist—the Back-fall, the Elevation, the Relish, the Slide, or the Springer. Between 1651 and 1702 no less than two hundred and fifty song-books were published in London. Most of the songs I have included in this book recur again and again in those collections, set to music by such composers as Dr. Blow, John Eccles, Henry Lawes, and Henry and Daniel Purcell.

Music, indeed, was no less an inspiration to the poets of the Restoration than love. The courtship of the two yielded a literature which, though it may rest a little below the peaks of lyrical achievement, has yet a lingering beauty of phrase and an undying reality for the restless heart. The swains who dallied with their nymphs beneath the willow trees, the gallants who ogled orange girls in the Pit, the goddesses who 'gave ambrosia in a kiss', or the ageing sceptics who simply asked 'to love and live in quiet'—all were students at that Academy of Compliments which taught them to shape their passions in gracious words and sing them to the music of the viol, the harpsichord, or the lute.

ACKNOWLEDGEMENTS

I CANNOT hope that this companion volume to my *Georgian Love Songs* will add more than a few trimmings to the great fabric of seventeenth-century scholarship. My aim has been to gather together, and arrange in chronological order of publication (grouping together the work of each poet), a representative selection of love lyrics of the period 1660–1714. If, in so doing, I have brought one or two minor poets and anonymous lyrics out of the shadows, and given a more general view of a literary landscape in which four or five notable figures have hitherto been the conspicuous features, I am content.

The compilation of a book such as this is only made possible by the research of those who have gone before, most notably the late Norman Ault, whose *Seventeenth Century Lyrics* (revised edition, 1950) is one of the monumental anthologies of our time. William Kerr's *Restoration Verse* (1930) has also been of great value. I have made much use of Professor V. de Sola Pinto's edition of Sedley's works (1928) and Mr. John Hayward's edition of Rochester (1926). I also express my special indebtedness to F. W. Galpin's *Old English Instruments of Music* (1910), Mr. Peter Quennell's *Aspects of Seventeenth Century Verse* (1933), Professor V. de Sola Pinto's life of *Sir Charles Sedley* (1927), and Mr. Arthur Bryant's *King Charles II* (1931). The bibliographical part of my work would have been impossible but for Day and Murrie's *English Song-Books, 1651–1702* (1940) and A. E. Case's *English Poetical Miscellanies, 1521–1750* (1935).

Again I express my thanks to Mr. Laurence Whistler for allowing the collection to be decorated with drawings by the late Rex Whistler which have not hitherto been published in book form.

After I was Married, and had brought My Wife Home to Cambridge; It so fell out, that one Rainy Morning I stay'd within; and in My Chamber, My Wife and I were all alone; She intent upon Her Needle-works, and I Playing upon my Lute at the Table by Her; She sat very Still, and Quiet, Listning to All I Played without a Word a Long Time, till at last, I hapned to Play This Lesson; which, so soon as I had once Play'd, She Earnestly desired Me to Play it again; For, said She, That shall be Called My Lesson. From which Words, so spoken, with Emphasis, and Accent, It presently came into my Remembrance, the Time when, and the Occasion of Its being produced, and return'd Her This Answer, viz. That it may very properly be call'd Your Lesson, for when I Compos'd It You were wholly in My Fancy, and the Chief Object and Ruler of My Thoughts.

THOMAS MACE, *Musick's Monument*, 1676

AFTER I was Married, and had brought My Wife Home to Cambridge, it so fell out that one Rainy Morning I stay'd within and in My Chamber. My Wife and I were all alone, She Intent upon Her Needle-works and I Playing upon my Lute at the Table by Her. She sat very Still and Quiet, Listning to All I Played without a Word a Long Time, till at last I hapned to Play This Lesson; which, so soon as I had once Play'd, She Earnestly desired Me to Play It again; For, said She, That shall be Called My Lesson. From which Words, so spoken, with Emphasis and Accent, It presently came into my Remembrance, the Time when, and the Occasion of Its being produced, and return'd Her This Answer, viz. That it may very properly be call'd Your Lesson, for when I Compos'd It You were wholly in My Fancy and the Chief Object and Ruler of My Thoughts.

—THOMAS MACE, *Musick's Monument*, 1676

VENUS

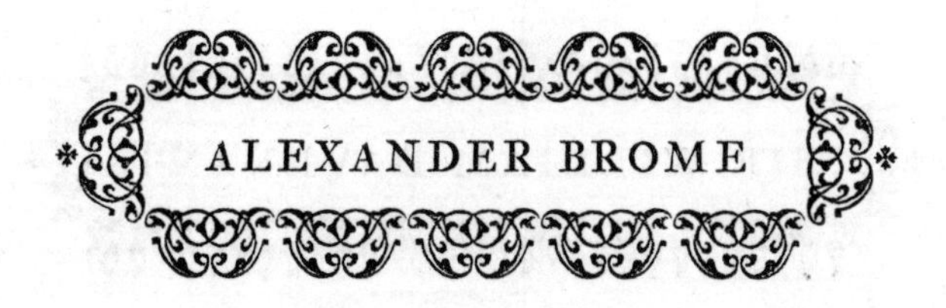

ALEXANDER BROME

I. *A Mock Song*

'Tis true, I never was in love:
  But now I mean to be;
    For there's no art
    Can shield a heart
From love's supremacie.

Though in my nonage I have seen
  A world of taking faces,
I had not age nor wit to ken
  Their several hidden graces.

Those virtues, which, though thinly set,
  In others are admired,
In thee are altogether met,
  Which make thee so desired,

That though I never was in love,
  Nor never meant to be,
    Thy self and parts,
    Above my arts,
Have drawn my heart to thee.

2

UNDER the willow shades they were
Free from the eye-sight of the sun,
For no intruding beam could there
Peep through to spy what things were done:
Thus shelter'd, they unseen did lye,
Surfeiting on each other's eye;
Defended by the willow shades alone,
The sun's heat they defy'd, and cool'd their own.

Whilst they did embrace unspy'd,
The conscious willows seem'd to smile,
That they with privacy supply'd,
Holding the door, as 'twere, the while,
And, when their dalliances were or'e,
The willows, to oblige 'em more,
Bowing, did seem to say, as they withdrew,
We can supply you with a cradle, too.

SIR GEORGE ETHEREGE

3

LADIES, though to your conqu'ring eyes
Love owes his chiefest victories,
And borrows those bright arms from you
With which he does the world subdue,
  Yet you your selves are not above
  The empire nor the griefs of love.

Then wrack not lovers with disdain,
Lest love on you revenge their pain;
You are not free because y'are fair;
The Boy did not his Mother spare:
  Beauty's but an offensive dart;
  It is no armour for the heart.

4

CLORIS, it is not in our pow'r
To say how long our love will last;
It may be we within this hour
May lose those joys we now may tast:
The blessed, that immortal be,
From change in love are only free.

And, though you now immortal seem,
Such is th'exactness of your frame,
Those that your beauty so esteem
Will find it cannot last the same:
Love from your eyes has stol'n my fire,
As apt to wast and to expire.

Then, since we mortal lovers are,
Let's question not how long 'twill last,
But while we love let us take care
Each minute be with pleasure past:
It were a madness to deny
To live because w'are sure to die.

Fear not, though love and beauty fail,
My reason shall my heart direct;
Your kindness now will then prevail,
And passion turn into respect:
CLORIS, at worst you'll in the end
But change your lover for a friend.

5. *The Faire but Cruel Girle*

THE nymph that undoes me is fair and unkind,
No lesse than a wonder by nature design'd;
She's the grief of my heart, but joy of my eye,
The cause of my flame, that never can dye.

Her lips, from whence wit obligingly flowes,
Have the colour of cherryes and smell of the rose;
Love and destiny both attend on her will;
She saves with a smile, with a frown she can kill.

The desperate lover can hope no redresse,
Where beauty and rigour are both in excesse;
In CAELIA they meet, so unhappy am I;
Who sees her must love; who loves her must die.

SIR GEORGE ETHEREGE

6

TELL me no more I am deceiv'd
While SYLVIA seems so kind,
And takes such care to be believ'd;
The cheat I fear to find:
To flatter me should falshood lye
Conceal'd in her soft youth,
A thousand times I'd rather dye
Than see th'unhappy truth.

My love all malice shall outbrave;
Let fops in libels rail;
If she th'appearances will save,
No scandal can prevail:
She makes me think I have her heart;
How much for that is due?
Tho' she but act the tender part,
The joy she gives is true.

7

YE happy swains, whose hearts are free
    From Love's imperial chain,
Take warning, and be taught by me
    T'avoid th'inchanting pain:
Fatal the wolves to trembling flocks,
    Fierce winds to blossoms prove;
To careless sea-men, hidden rocks,
    To human quiet, Love.

Fly the fair sex if bliss you prize;
    The snake's beneath the flow'r:
Who ever gaz'd on beauteous eyes
    That tasted quiet more?
How faithless is the lovers' joy!
    How constant is their care!
The kind with falshood do destroy;
    The cruel, with despair.

8. *Secret Love*

I FEED a flame within which so torments me
That it both pains my heart, and yet contents me:
'Tis such a pleasing smart, and I so love it,
That I had rather die than once remove it.

Yet he for whom I grieve shall never know it,
My tongue does not betray, nor my eyes show it:
Not a sigh nor a tear my pain discloses;
But they fall silently like dew on roses.

Thus to prevent my love from being cruel,
My heart's the sacrifice, as 'tis the fuel:
And while I suffer this to give him quiet,
My faith rewards my love, though he deny it.

On his eyes will I gaze, and there delight me;
While I conceal my love, no frown can fright me:
To be more happy I dare not aspire;
Nor can I fall more low, mounting no higher.

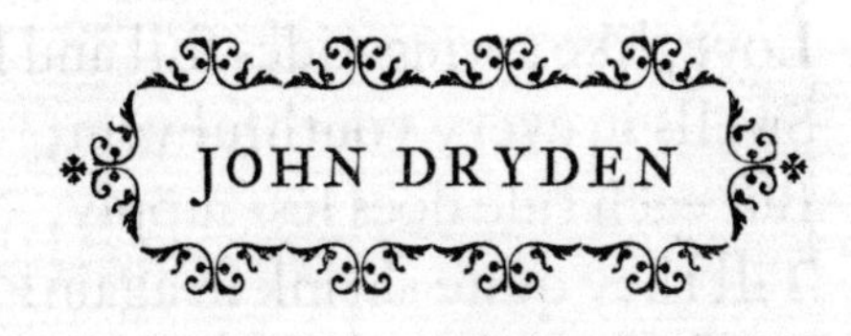

9

Ah, how sweet it is to love!
Ah, how gay is young desire!
And what pleasing pains we prove
When we first approach love's fire!
  Pains of love be sweeter far
  Than all other pleasures are.

Sighs which are from lovers blown
Do but gently heave the heart:
Ev'n the tears they shed alone
Cure, like trickling balm, their smart.
  Lovers, when they lose their breath,
  Bleed away in easie death.

Love and time with reverence use,
Treat 'em like a parting friend;
Nor the golden gifts refuse,
Which in youth sincere they send;
  For each year their price is more,
  And they less simple than before.

Love, like spring-tides full and high,
Swells in every youthful vein;
But each tide does less supply,
Till they quite shrink in again:
  If a flow in age appear,
  'Tis but rain, and runs not clear.

10

FARWELL, ungratefull traytor,
  Farwell, my perjur'd swain;
Let never injur'd creature
  Believe a man again.
The pleasure of possessing
Surpasses all expressing,
But 'tis too short a blessing,
  And love too long a pain.

'Tis easie to deceive us
  In pity of your pain,
But when we love you leave us
  To rail at you in vain.
Before we have descry'd it,
There is no bliss beside it,
But she that once has try'd it
  Will never love again.

The passion you pretended
  Was onely to obtain;
But when the charm is ended
  The charmer you disdain.
Your love by ours we measure,
Till we have lost our treasure;
But dying is a pleasure
  When living is a pain.

II

AFTER the pangs of a desperate lover,
When day and night I have sigh'd all in vain,
Ah what a pleasure it is to discover
In her eyes pity, who causes my pain!

When with unkindness our love at a stand is,
And both have punish'd our selves with the pain,
Ah what a pleasure the touch of her hand is!
Ah what a pleasure to press it again!

When the denyal comes fainter and fainter,
And her eyes give what her tongue does deny,
Ah what a trembling I feel when I venture!
Ah what a trembling does usher my joy!

When, with a sigh, she accords me the blessing,
And her eyes twinkle 'twixt pleasure and pain,
Ah what a joy 'tis, beyond all expressing!
Ah what a joy to hear, *Shall we again?*

12

No, no, poor suff'ring heart, no change endeavour;
Choose to sustain the smart, rather than leave her.
My ravish'd eyes behold such charms about her,
I can dye with her, but not live without her:
One tender sigh of hers, to see me languish,
Will more than pay the price of my past anguish:
Beware, oh cruel Fair, how you smile on me!
'Twas a kind look of yours that has undone me.

Love has in store for me one happy minute,
And she will end my pain who did begin it;
Then no day void of bliss or pleasure leaving,
Ages shall slide away without perceiving:
CUPID shall guard the door, the more to please us,
And keep out Time and Death, when they would
seize us:
Time and Death shall depart, and say, in flying,
Love has found out a way to live by dying.

13

ANONYMOUS

13

I SERVE AMYNTA whiter than the snow,
  Streighter than cedar, brighter than the glass,
More fine in trip than foot of running roe,
  More pleasant than the field of flow'ring grass,
More gladsom to my with'ring joys that fade
  Than winter's sun, or summer's cooling shade.

Sweeter than swelling grape of ripest vine,
  Softer than feathers of the fairest swan,
Smoother than jet, more stately than the pine,
  Fresher than poplar, smaller than my span,
Clearer than PHOEBUS' fiery pointed beam,
  Or icy crust of crystal's frozen stream.

Yet is she curster than the bear by kind,
  And harder-hearted than the aged oak,
More glib than oyl, more fickle than the wind,
  More stiff than steel, no sooner bent but broke:
Lo, thus my service is a lasting sore;
  Yet will I serve, although I die therefore.

14. *The First Song in the Ball at Court*

I PASS all my hours in a shady old grove,
And I live not the day that I see not my love:
I survey every walk now my PHILLIS is gone,
And sigh when I think we were there all alone:
  O then 'tis, O then, I think there's no such Hell
  Like loving, like loving too well.

But each shade and each conscious bow'r that I find,
Where I once have been happy, & she has been kind,
And I see the print left of her shape in the green,
And imagine the pleasure may yet come agen,
  O then 'tis, O then, I think no joy's above
  The pleasures, the pleasures of love.

While alone to my self I repeat all her charms,
She I love may be lock'd in another man's armes:
She may laugh at my cares, and so false she may be,
To say all the kind things she before said to me:
  O then 'tis, O then, I think there's no such Hell
  Like loving, like loving too well.

But when I consider the truth of her heart,
Such an innocent passion, so kind, without art,
I fear I have wrong'd her, and hope she may be
So full of true love, to be jealous of me:
  O then 'tis, O then, I think no joy's above
  The pleasures, the pleasures of love.

SIR CHARLES SEDLEY

15

Ah Cloris! that I now could sit
  As unconcern'd as when
Your infant beauty cou'd beget
  No pleasure nor no pain.

When I the dawn us'd to admire,
  And prais'd the coming day,
I little thought the growing fire
  Must take my rest away.

Your charms in harmless childhood lay
  Like metals in the mine;
Age from no face took more away
  Then youth conceal'd in thine.

But, as your charms insensibly
  To their perfection prest,
Fond love as unperceiv'd did flye,
  And in my bosom rest.

My passion with your beauty grew,
  And CUPID at my heart,
Still as his mother favour'd you,
  Threw a new flaming dart.

Each glori'd in their wanton part;
  To make a lover he
Employ'd the utmost of his art,
  To make a beauty she.

Though now I slowly bend to love,
  Uncertain of my fate,
If your fair self my chains approve,
  I shall my freedom hate.

Lovers, like dying men, may well
  At first disorder'd be,
Since none alive can truly tell
  What fortune they must see.

16. *To Cloris*

Cloris, I cannot say your eyes
Did my unwary heart surprize;
Nor will I swear it was your face,
Your shape, or any nameless grace;
For you are so intirely fair,
To love a part, injustice were;
No drowning man can know which drop
Of water his last breath did stop;
So, when the stars in heaven appear,
And joyn to make the night look clear,
The light we no one's bounty call,
But the obliging gift of all.
He that does lips or hands adore
Deserves them only, and no more;
But I love all and every part,
And nothing less can ease my heart.
Cupid that lover weakly strikes
Who can express what 'tis he likes.

17. *To Cloris*

Cloris, I justly am betray'd
By a design my self had laid,
Like an old rook, whom in his cheat
A run of fortune does defeat:
I thought at first with a small sum
Of love thy heap to overcome,
Presuming on thy want of art,
Thy gentle and unpractis'd heart;
But naked beauty can prevail
Like open force, when all things fail:
Instead of that thou hast all mine,
And I have not one stake of thine;
And, like all winners, do'st discover
A willingness to give me over;
And, though I beg thou wilt not now,
'Twere better thou should'st do so too;
For I so far in debt shall run,
Even thee I shall be forc'd to shun:
My hand, alas, is no more mine,
Else it had long ago been thine;
My heart I give thee, and we call
No man unjust that parts with all.

18

GET you gone, you will undo me,
If you love me don't pursue me;
Let that inclination perish
Which I dare no longer cherish.
With harmless thoughts I did begin,
But in the crowd love entred in;
I knew him not, he was so gay,
So innocent and full of play.
At every hour, in every place,
I either saw or form'd your face;
All that in plays was finely writ
Fancy for you and me did fit;
My dreams at night were all of you,
Such as till then I never knew.
I sported thus with young desire,
Never intending to go higher;
But now his teeth and claws are grown,
Let me the fatal lion shun.
You found me harmless; leave me so;
For, were I not, you'd leave me too.

19

PHILLIS, let's shun the common fate,
And let our love ne'r turn to hate.
I'll dote no longer then I can,
Without being call'd a faithless man.
When we begin to want discourse,
And kindness seems to tast of force,
As freely as we met we'll part,
Each one possest of their own heart.
Thus, whilst rash fools themselves undo,
We'll game, and give off savers too.
So equally the match we'll make,
Both shall be glad to draw the stake.
A smile of thine shall make my bliss;
I will enjoy thee in a kiss.
If from this height our kindness fall,
We'll bravely scorn to love at all.
If thy affection first decay,
I will the blame on nature lay.
Alas, what cordial can remove
The hasty fate of dying love?
Thus we will all the world excel
In loving and in parting well.

20

LOVE still has somthing of the sea,
From whence his mother rose;
No time his slaves from doubt can free,
Nor give their thoughts repose.

They are becalm'd in clearest days,
And in rough weather tost;
They wither under cold delays,
Or are in tempests lost.

One while they seem to touch the port,
Then straight into the main
Some angry wind in cruel sport
The vessel drives again.

At first disdain and pride they fear,
Which, if they chance to 'scape,
Rivals and falshood soon appear,
In a more dreadful shape.

By such degrees to joy they come,
And are so long withstood,
So slowly they receive the sum,
It hardly does them good.

'Tis cruel to prolong a pain,
And to defer a joy;
Believe me, gentle CELEMENE
Offends the wingèd boy.

An hundred thousand oaths your fears
Perhaps would not remove;
And, if I gaz'd a thousand years,
I could no deeper love.

SIR CHARLES SEDLEY

21

Not, Celia, that I juster am,
  Or better than the rest;
For I would change each hour, like them,
  Were not my heart at rest.

But I am ty'd to very thee
  By every thought I have;
Thy face I only care to see,
  Thy heart I only crave.

All that in woman is ador'd
  In thy dear self I find;
For the whole sex can but afford
  The handsome and the kind.

Why then should I seek farther store,
  And still make love a-new?
When change itself can give no more
  'Tis easie to be true.

22

PHILLIS, men say that all my vows
Are to thy fortune paid;
Alas! my heart he little knows
Who thinks my love a trade.

Were I of all these woods the lord,
One berry from thy hand
More real pleasure would afford
Than all my large command.

My humble love has learnt to live
On what the nicest maid
Without a conscious blush may give
Beneath the myrtle-shade.

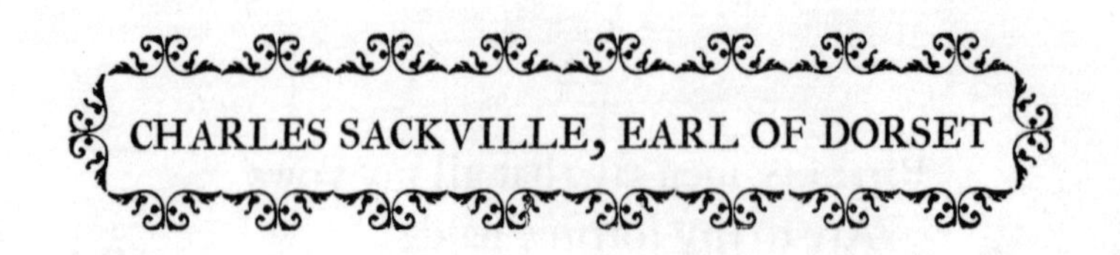

CHARLES SACKVILLE, EARL OF DORSET

23

Phyllis, for shame, let us improve,
  A thousand several ways,
These few short minutes stol'n by love
  From many tedious days.

Whilst you want courage to despise
  The censure of the grave,
For all the tyrants in your eyes,
  Your heart is but a slave.

My love is full of noble pride,
  And never will submit
To let that fop Discretion ride
  In triumph over Wit.

False friends I have, as well as you,
  That daily counsel me
Vain friv'lous trifles to pursue,
  And leave off loving thee.

When I the least belief bestow
 On what such fools advise,
May I be dull enough to grow
 Most miserably wise.

24

MAY the ambitious pleasure find
 In crowds and empty noise,
While gentle love does fill my mind
 With silent real joys.

Let knave and fool grow rich and cruel,
 And the world think 'em wise,
While I lye dying at her feet,
 And all that world despise.

Let conqu'ring kings new trophies raise,
 And melt in Court-delights;
Her eyes can give me brighter days,
 Her arms much softer nights.

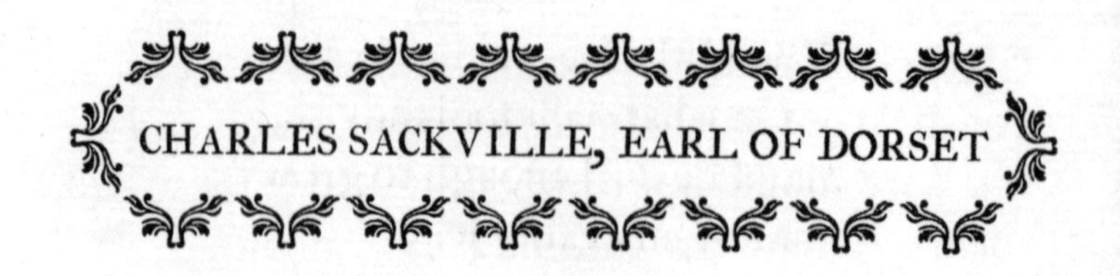

CHARLES SACKVILLE, EARL OF DORSET

25

METHINKS the poor town has been troubled too long
With PHILLIS and CLORIS in every song,
By fools who at once can both love and despair,
And will never leave calling them cruel and fair;
Which justly provokes me in rhime to express
The truth that I know of bonny BLACK BESS.

This BESS of my heart, this BESS of my soul,
Has a skin white as milk, and hair black as cole;
She's plump, yet with ease you may span round her waste,
But her round swelling thighs can scarce be embraste;
Her belly is soft; not a word of the rest;
But I know what I think when I drink to the best.

The ploughman and squire, the erranter clown,
At home she subdu'd in her paragon gown;
But now she adornes the Boxes and Pit,
And the proudest town gallants are forc'd to submit;
All hearts fall a leaping wherever she comes,
And beat day and night, like my LORD CRAVEN's drums.

I dare not permit her to come to WHITEHALL,
For she'd out-shine the ladies, paint, jewels and all:
If a Lord should but whisper his love in the croud,
She'd sell him a bargain and laugh out aloud;
Then the QUEEN, overhearing what BETTY did
say,
Would send Mr. ROPER to take her away.

But to these that have had my dear BESS in their
arms
She's gentle and knows how to soften her charms,
And to every beauty can add a new grace,
Having learn'd how to lisp and to trip in her pace,
And, with head on one side and a languishing eye,
To kill *us* by looking as if *she* would dye.

26

DORINDA'S sparkling wit and eyes,
Uniting, cast too fierce a light,
Which blazes high, but quickly dyes,
Pains not the heart, but hurts the eyes.

Love is a calmer gentle joy;
Smooth are his looks, and soft his pace;
Her CUPID is a black-guard boy,
That runs his link full in your face.

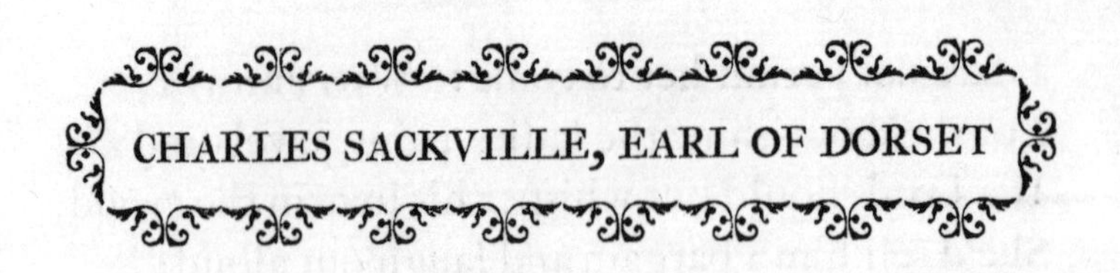

27

THE fire of love in youthful blood,
Like what is kindled in brush-wood,
    But for a moment burns;
Yet in that moment makes a mighty noise,
It crackles, and to vapour turns,
    And soon it self destroys.

But, when crept into aged veins,
It slowly burns, and long remains,
    And, with a sullen heat,
Like fire in logs, it glows and warms 'em long,
And, though the flame be not so great,
    Yet is the heat as strong.

ANONYMOUS

28

Oh! the time that is past,
When she held me so fast,
And declar'd that her honour no longer cou'd last:
No light but her languishing eyes did appear,
To prevent all excuses of blushing and fear.

When she sigh'd and unlac'd
With such trembling and haste,
As if she had long'd to be closer embrac'd!
My lips the sweet pleasure of kisses enjoy'd,
While my hands were in search of hid treasure employ'd.

With my heart all on fire
In the flames of desire,
I boldly pursu'd what she seem'd to require:
She cry'd: *Oh, for pity's sake! change your ill mind:*
Pray, Amyntas, *be civil, or I'le be unkind.*

All your bliss you destroy,
Like a naked young boy,
Who fears the kind river he came to enjoy . . .
Let's in, my dear CLORIS! *I'le save thee from harm,*
And make the cold element pleasant and warm.

Dear AMYNTAS! she cryes;
Then she casts down her eyes,
And with kisses consents what she faintly denies:
Too sure of my conquest, I purpose to stay
Till her freer consent did more sweeten the prey.

But too late I begun;
For her passion was done:
Now, AMYNTAS, she cryes, *I will never be won:*
Thy tears and thy courtship no pity can move;
Thou hast slighted the critical minute of love.

29

AT the sight of my PHILLIS, from every part
A spring-tide of joy does flow up to my heart,
That quickens each pulse and swells every vein;
But all my delights are still mingled with pain.

So strange a distemper sure love cannot bring;
To my knowledge love was a quieter thing,
So gentle and tame that he never was known
So much as to wake me when I lay alone.

But the boy is much grown, and so alter'd of late,
Hee's become a more furious passion than hate;
Since by PHILLIS restor'd to the Empire of hearts,
He has new strung his bow, and sharpen'd his darts,
And, strictly the rites of his Crown to maintain,
He breaks every heart, and turns every brain.

My madness, alass, I too plainly discover;
For he is at least as much madman as lover,
Who, for one cruel beauty, is ready to quit
All the nymphs of the Stage and those of the Pitt,
The joyes of Hide-Park and the Mall's dear delight,
To live sober all day and chast all the night.

ANONYMOUS

30

WHEN first my free heart was surpriz'd by desire,
So soft was the wound, and so gentle the fire,
My sighes were so sweet, and so pleasant the smart,
I pitty'd the slave who had ne'r lost his heart:
He thinks himself happy and free, but alas!
He is far from that heaven which lovers possess.

In Nature was nothing that I could compare
With the beauty of PHILLIS, I thought her so fair:
A wit so divine all her sayings did fill;
A Goddess she seem'd, and I mention'd her still
With a zeal more inflam'd, and a passion more true,
Than a martyr in flames for religion can shew.

More vertues and graces I found in her mind
Then schooles can invent or the Gods e're design'd;
She seem'd to be mine by each glance of her eye
(If mortals might aim at a blessing so high):
Each day, with new favours, new hopes she did give;
But alas! what is wish'd we too soon do beleive.

With awful respect while I lov'd and admir'd,
But fear'd to attempt what so much I desir'd,
How soon were my hopes and my heaven destroy'd!
A shepherd more daring fell on and enjoy'd:
Yet, in spite of ill fate and the pains I endure,
I will find a new PHILLIS to give me a cure.

31

To her beauty I'le pay
My devotions each day;
That all jaunty delights will me give:
Though her soul do expire,
PHOENIX-like in love's fire,
Yet again her enjoyments do live.

With a brisk aerie spark,
At Spring Garden or Park,
In glass coach or balcony thus free,
She will vanquish all hearts,
With her boon meen and parts;
Shee's the heaven on earth unto me.

32

PHILLIS, the time is come that we must sever;
Long we have linger'd 'twixt kindness and strife;
And, though we have promis'd our selves to love
ever,
Yet there 's a fate in love, as well as life:
So many jealousies dayly we try,
Sometimes we freeze, and sometimes we fry,
That love in colds or feavours will dye.

Both by our selves and others tormented,
Still in suspence betwixt heaven and hell,
Ever desiring, and never contented,
Either not loving, or loving too well;
Parting we still are in each other's powers;
Our love 's a weather of sun-shine and show'rs;
Its dayes are bitter, though sweet are its hours.

Why should we Fate any longer importune,
Since to each other unhappy we prove?
Like losing gamesters we tempt our ill fortune;
Both might be luckier in a new love:
This were the way our reason bear sway;
But when we so pleasing a passion destroy,
We may be more happy, but less should enjoy.

33

PEACE, CUPID! take thy bow in hand;
I'th' gloomy shade in ambush stand,
To watch a cruel nymph frequents this bow'r,
Cold as the streams, but sweeter than each flow'r.
There, there she is! direct thy dart
Into that stony marble heart:
Draw, quickly draw, and shew thy art.
Wo's me! thou art blind indeed, thou hast shot *me*!
Whiles she 'scapes in the Grove, and laughs at thee;
And laughs, &c.

ANONYMOUS

34

AH! cruel eyes, that first enflam'd
My poor resistless heart,
That when I would my thoughts have blam'd
They still encrease the smart.
What pow'r above
Creates such love,
To languish with desire?
May some disdain
Encrease my pain,
Or may the flame expire!

And yet I dye to think how soon
My wishes may return:
If slighted, and my hope once gone,
I must in silence mourn.
Then, tyranness,
Do but express
The mystery of your pow'r;
'Tis as soon said,
You'l love and wed,
As studying for't an hour.

I yield to Fate, though your fair eyes
Have made the pow'r your own;
'Twas they did first my heart surprize;
Dear nymph! 'twas they alone.
For honour's sake,
Your heart awake,
And let your pitty move,
Lest in despair
Of one so fair
I bid adieu to love.

35. *Chorus*

MANY thousand follys are
The unhappy lover's share:
Doubtful pangs and wild desires,
Immod'rate heat, unruly fires,
Tides of relenting and disdain,
Quiv'ring rapture, joy and pain;
But, with these fantastick things,
Love many true perfections brings.

36

Dear Aminda, in vain you so coily refuse
What nature and love do inspire;
That formal old way which your mother did use
Can never confine the desire;
It rather adds oyl to the fire.

When the tempting delights of wooing are lost,
And pleasures a duty become,
We both shall appear, like some dead lover's ghost,
To frighten each other from home,
And the genial bed like a tombe.

Now, low at your feet your fond lover will lye,
And seek a new fate in your eyes;
One amorous smile will exalt him so high
He can all but Aminda despise;
Then change to a frown, and he dies.

To love and each other we'll ever be true;
  But, to raise our enjoyments by art,
We'll often fall out, and as often renew,
  For to wound and to cure the smart
  Is the pleasure which captives the heart.

37

AMYNTAS led me to a grove
Where all the trees did shade us:
The sun itself, though it had strove,
Yet could not have betray'd us.
The place, secure from humane eyes,
No other fear allows,
But when the winds that gently rise
Do kiss the yielding boughs.

Down there we sat upon the moss,
And did begin to play
A thousand wanton tricks, to pass
The heat of all the day.
A many kisses he did give,
And I return'd the same,
Which made me willing to receive
That which I dare not name.

His charming eyes no aid requir'd,
To tell their amorous tale;
On her that was already fir'd
'Twas easie to prevail.
He did but kiss and clasp me round,
Whilst they his thoughts exprest,
And laid me gently on the ground;
Ah, who can guess the rest?

APHRA BEHN

38

LOVE in phantastique triumph sat,
Whilst bleeding hearts around him flow'd,
For whom fresh pains he did create,
And strange tyrannick pow'r he shew'd:
From thy bright eyes he took his fires,
Which round about in sport he hurl'd,
But 'twas from mine he took desires
Enough t'undoe the amorous world.

From me he took his sighs and tears,
From thee his pride and cruelty;
From me his languishments and fears,
And ev'ry killing dart from thee:
Thus thou and I the God have arm'd,
And set him up a deity;
But my poor heart alone is harm'd,
Whilst thine the victor is, and free.

THOMAS FLATMAN

39

BE not too proud, imperious dame,
Your charmes are transitory things,
May melt while you at heaven aim,
Like ICARUS' waxen wings,
And you a part in his misfortunes beare,
Drown'd in a briny ocean of despaire.

You think your beauties are above
The poet's brain, the painter's hand,
As if upon the throne of love
You only should the world command;
Yet know, though you presume your title true,
There are pretenders that will rival you.

There 's an experienc'd rebel, Time,
And, in his squadarns, Poverty;
There 's Age, that brings along with him
A terrible artillery;
And, if against all these thou keep'st thy crown,
Th'usurper Death will make thee lay it down.

40. *Bathing Her Self*

HAPPY this wand'ring stream!
Which gently proud does seem,
As it had ne're before
So rich a burthen bore.

Swell'd with her body now,
It does with joy o'reflow.
Th'exulting waves forget
The limits to them set;
With joy now swelling more
Then e're with rage before,
Her breast yet lightly raise
To measure its smooth waies,
While her soft arms divide
The current on each side,
Which, in new circles broke
By ev'ry bending stroke,
Thus troubled does appear
As strook with sun-beams clear.

From out of water n'ere
Did rise a shape so fair;
Nor could it e're to sight
Reflect a form so bright:
Such sweetness, nor such grace,
Shin'd not in VENUS' face,
When froth did it enclose,
As 'bove the waves it rose,
And in white circles crown'd
The whiter goddess round:
Less pleasing she did shew
Her naked glories new,
Though all the deep then smil'd
To see the sea-born child.

No undisturbed brook,
In which th'heav'ns chuse to look,
Sees such a beauty move
As this reflects above;
No deeps such treasures know,
As what this hides below.

41. *Fanning Her Self*

SEE how the charming fair
Does break the yielding air,
Which, by her troubled so,
More pure, more smooth, does flow.
Winds without murmurs rise,
Complaining in sad sighs,
Though they dare not repine
How loth they're to resign
Their int'rest in the fair
To new succeeding air.
How silently they grieve,
Their snatch't embrace to leave
To new winds, who their place
Supply, and their embrace,
Courting their longer bliss
At ev'ry parting kiss,
While, with a gentle gale,
They swell her painted sail.
Then, trembling, they give way,
Fearing to disobey,

Though fain they her would bear
With ev'ry moving air.
In vain, alas! they prove
Unkindness to remove;
In vain to win the field;
Air may, she cannot, yield.
Her hand a thousand waies
New favourites does raise,
Which, to salute her proud,
Do round about her croud,
And rival-like pursue
Th'old, thrust out by the new.

Well may they boast they can
Move false trees, in her fanne,
And with their tremblings make
Their trunks, though rooted, shake.
With oaks they may contend,
But she can never bend.
She, should ev'n storms engage
Her with their roughest rage,
And all their utmost prove,
Too stubborn is to move.

RICHARD LEIGH

42

Seeing Her in a Balcone

THE sun at his first rising so,
Gilding some mountain-top, does show,
  Illuminating all below,

  As she does from on high appear,
And with like glory crowns her sphere,
Enlightning her horizon here,

Above those dark'ning shadows plac't,
Which lower house-tops round us cast,
That usher night e're day be past,

The proper seat, and only scene
Of all things fair and all serene,
Which nearest heaven still are seen.

Our wingèd thoughts, in their bold flight,
Out-fly not yet our raisèd sight,
Nor ever soar a braver height.

Upwards our eyes can nought pursue
Beyond what we now boast in view,
While we look up to heav'n and you.

Vouchsafe then (fair one) to allow
That we, whom Fate has plac'd below,
To our divinity may bow.

And, though beneath your feet we bend,
Permit our eyes but to ascend;
Further our hopes dare not pretend.

THOMAS DUFFETT

43

I SIGH'D and I writ
And imploy'd all my wit,
And still pretty SILVIA deny'd;
'Twas virtue, I thought,
And became such a sot,
I ador'd her the more for her pride.

Till, mask'd in the Pit,
My coy LUCRECE I met;
A croud of gay fops held her play;
So brisk and so free,
With her smart repartee,
I was cur'd and went blushing away.

Poor lovers mistake
The addresses they make,
With vows to be constant and true;
Though all the nymphs hold
For the sport that is old;
Yet their play-mates must ever be new.

Each pretty new toy
They would dye to enjoy,
And then for a newer they pine;
But when they perceive
Others like what they leave,
They will cry for their bauble agen.

44

UNTO a feast I will invite thee,
Where various dishes shall delight thee;
The steeming vapours drawn up hot
From earth, that Nature's porridge-pot,
Shall be our broth; we'll drink, my dear,
The thinner air for our small beer;
And if thou lik'st it not I'le call aloud,
And make our butler broach a cloud;
Of paler planets, for thy sake,
White-pots and trembling custards make;
The twinkling stars shall to our wish
Make a grand salad in a dish;
Snow for our sugar shall not fail,
Fine candid ice, comfits of hail;
For oranges, gilt clouds we'll squeeze,
The milky way we'll turn to cheese;
Sun-beams we'l catch shall stand in place
Of hotter ginger, nutmegs, mace;

Sun-setting clouds for roses sweet,
And violet skies strow'd for our feet;
The sphears shall for our musick play,
While spirits dance the time away;
When we drink healths JOVE shall be proud,
Th'old Cannoneer, to fire a cloud,
That all the Gods may know our mirth,
And trembling mortals, too, on earth;
And when our feasting shall be done
I'll lead thee up hill to the sun,
And place thee there that thy eyes may
Add greater lustre to the day.

ANONYMOUS

45

I LIK'D but never lov'd before
  I saw that charming face;
Now every feature I adore,
  And dote on ev'ry grace.

She ne'er shall know that kind desire
  Which her cold look denys,
Unless my heart, that 's all on fire,
  Should sparkle through my eyes.

Then, if no gentle glance return
  A silent leave to speak,
My heart, which would for ever burn,
  Alas! must sigh and break.

46

More love or more disdain I crave;
Sweet, be not still indifferent:
Oh! send me quickly to my grave,
Or else afford me more content;
  Or love or hate me more or less,
  For love abhors all lukewarmness.

Give me a tempest, if 'twill drive
Me to the place where I would be;
Or, if you'l have me still alive,
Confess you will be kind to me.
  Give hopes of bliss, or dig my grave;
  More love or more disdain I crave.

47

To one that asked me why I lov'd J.G.

WHY do I love? Go, ask the glorious sun
Why every day it round the world doth run;
Ask THAMES and TIBER why they ebb and flow;
Ask damask roses why in June they blow;
Ask ice and hail the reason why they're cold;
Decaying beauties, why they will grow old.
They'l tell thee Fate, that every thing doth move,
Inforces them to this, and me to love.
There is no reason for our love or hate;
'Tis irresistible, as death or fate.
'Tis not his face; I've sense enough to see
That is not good, though doated on by me;
Nor is't his tongue that has this conquest won,
For that at least is equall'd by my own:
His carriage can to none obliging be;
'Tis rude, affected, full of vanity,
Strangely ill-natur'd, peevish and unkind,
Unconstant, false, to jealousy inclin'd:
His temper cou'd not have so great a pow'r;
'Tis mutable, and changes every hour:

Those vigorous years that women so adore
Are past in him; he's twice my age, and more.
And yet I love this false, this worthless man
With all the passion that a woman can;
Doat on his imperfections; though I spy
Nothing to love, I love, and know not why:
Since 'tis decreed in the dark book of fate
That I shou'd love and he shou'd be ingrate.

48

KNOW, CELADON, in vain you use
These little arts to me:
Though STREPHON did my heart refuse,
I cannot give it thee:
His harsh refusal hath not brought
Its value yet so low
That what was worth that shepherd's thought
I shou'd on you bestow.

Nor can I love my STREPHON less
For his ungrateful pride,
Though honour does, I must confess,
My guilty passion chide.
That lovely youth I still adore,
Though now it be in vain;
But yet of him I ask no more
Than pity for my pain.

RICHARD DUKE

49

SEE what a conquest love has made!
Beneath the myrtle's am'rous shade
  The charming fair CORINNA lyes,
All melting in desire,
  Quenching in teares those flaming eyes
That set the world on fire.

What cannot teares and beauty doe!
The youth, by chance, stood by and knew
  For whom those chrystall streames did flow;
And, tho' he n'er before
  To her eyes' brightest rayes did bow,
Weeps too, and does adore.

So, when the heav'ns serene and cleare,
Gilded with gawdy light appeare,
  Each craggy rock and ev'ry stone
Their native rigour keep;
  But when in raine the clouds fall down
The hardest marbles weep.

50

AFTER the fiercest pangs of hot desire,
Between PANTHEA's rising breasts
His bending head PHILANDER rests,
Though vanquisht, yet unknowing to retire,
Close hugs the charmer, and, asham'd to yield,
Though he has lost the day, still keeps the field.

When, with a sigh, the fair PANTHEA said,
What pitty 'tis, ye gods, that all
The bravest warriors soonest fall!
Then, with a kiss, she gently rais'd his head,
Arm'd him again for fight, for nobly she
More loved the combate than the victory.

Then, more enrag'd for being beat before,
With all his strength he does prepare
More fiercely to renew the war;
Nor ceases till that noble prize he bore;
Ev'n her such wond'rous courage did surprize;
She hugs the dart that wounded her, and dyes.

51

Coy Clelia, veil those charming eyes,
From whose surprize there 's none can part;
For he that gazes surely dyes,
Or leaves behind a conquered heart.

I durst not once presume to look,
Or cast my wary eyes aside,
But, as a boy that cons his book,
Close sitting by his master's side,

Dares not presume to look awry
On toys that catch the wand'ring sense;
So, if I gaze, I surely die:
Against those charms there 's no defence.

Thus heathens, at the sun's up-rise,
Unto the ground did bow their head,
Not able with their feeble eyes
To view their God they worshippèd.

52. *On a Sigh*

Go, mournful sigh, haste to my fair,
And to her what thou know'st declare;
Tell her that thou wert so opprest
Within the prison of my breast,
That, having broak the gaol, thou fled'st to
her for rest.

But if unkindly she deny,
Then shall thy wretched gaoler die;
And by this means thou shalt be free
From thy confinement, she from thee,
And I from all my grief and wretched misery.

But yet, poor mournful breath, beware
Thou dost not draw from her a tear.
For if thou dost I will confine
Thee to this hollow breast of mine,
And give thee no more leave or time to wander
there.

For who can tell but she may be
So loving as to pitty thee,
And on thy sorrow notice take,
And entertain thee for my sake
In Paradice of joy and full felicity.

THOMAS D'URFEY

53. *To Cynthia*

ENAMOUR'D angels leave the sky
To hear the music of her tongue:
Fond Cupids round about her fly,
To kiss her as she walks along:
The trees all bow their verdant heads,
Like humble lovers, when she talks;
And blushing flowers deck the meads,
As proud they may adorn her walks.

She has such beauty as were fit
To bless the greatest monarch's side,
A mine of rich obliging wit
Without the least alloy of pride:
Tell me no more of joys above,
With which immortal souls are crown'd;
There is a rapture in her love
Which zealous bigots never found.

54

BORN with the vices of my kind,
  I should inconstant be,
Dear CELIA, could I rambling find
  More beauty than in thee:
The rouling surges of my blood,
  By virtue now grown low,
Should a new show'r encrease the flood,
  Too soon would overflow:
But frailty (when thy face I see)
  Does modestly retire;
Uncommon must her graces be
  Whose look can bound desire:
Not to my virtue but thy pow'r
  This constancy is due:
When change itself can give no more,
  'Tis easy to be true.

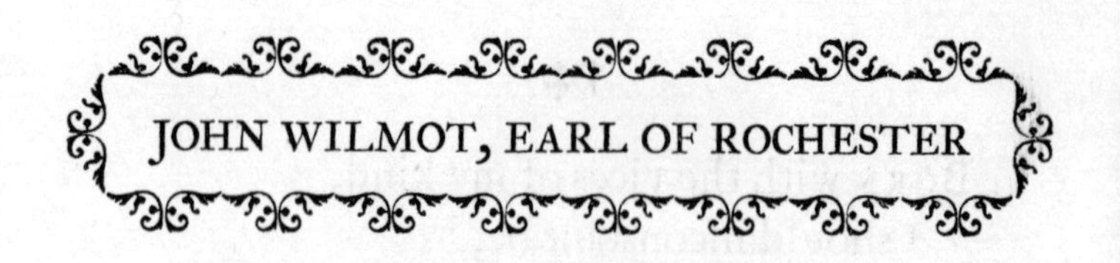

55

I CANNOT change, as others do,
Though you unjustly scorn:
Since that poor Swain that sighs for you
For you alone was born.
No, PHILIS, no, your heart to move
A surer way I'll try:
And, to revenge my slighted love,
Will still love on, will still love on, and die.

When, kill'd with grief, AMYNTAS lies,
And you to mind shall call
The sighs that now unpitied rise,
The tears that vainly fall;
That welcome hour that ends this smart,
Will then begin your pain;
For such a faithful tender heart
Can never break, can never break in vain.

56

ABSENT from thee, I languish still;
  Then ask me not, When I return?
The straying fool 'twill plainly kill
  To wish all day, all night to mourn.

Dear, from thine arms then let me flie,
  That my fantastick mind may prove
The torments it deserves to try,
  That tears my fixt heart from my Love.

When, wearied with a world of woe,
  To thy safe bosom I retire,
Where love and peace and truth does flow,
  May I contented there expire.

Lest, once more wand'ring from that Heav'n,
  I fall on some base heart unblest;
Faithless to thee, false, unforgiven,
  And lose my everlasting rest.

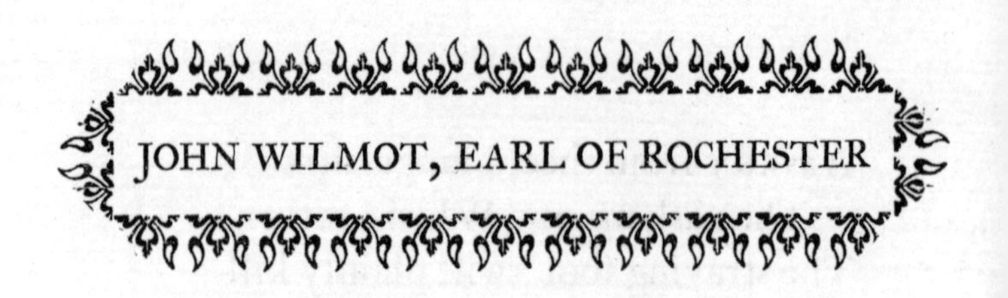

JOHN WILMOT, EARL OF ROCHESTER

57. *The Mistress*

An age in her embraces past
  Would seem a winter's day,
Where life and light with envious haste
  Are torn and snatch'd away.

But, oh! how slowly minutes roul,
  When absent from her eyes,
That fed my love, which is my soul;
  It languishes and dies.

For then, no more a soul but shade,
  It mournfully does move,
And haunts my breast, by absence made
  The living tomb of love.

You wiser men, despise me not,
  Whose love-sick fancy raves
On shades of souls, and Heav'n knows what;
  Short ages live in graves.

Whene'er those wounding eyes, so full
  Of sweetness, you did see,
Had you not been profoundly dull,
  You had gone mad like me.

Nor censure us, you who perceive
  My best belov'd and me,
Sigh and lament, complain and grieve;
  You think we disagree.

Alas! 'tis sacred jealousie,
  Love rais'd to an extream;
The only proof 'twixt them and me
  We love, and do not dream.

Fantastick fancies fondly move,
  And in frail joys believe,
Taking false pleasure for true love;
  But pain can ne'er deceive.

Kind jealous doubts, tormenting fears,
  And anxious cares, when past,
Prove our heart's treasure fix'd and dear,
  And make us blest at last.

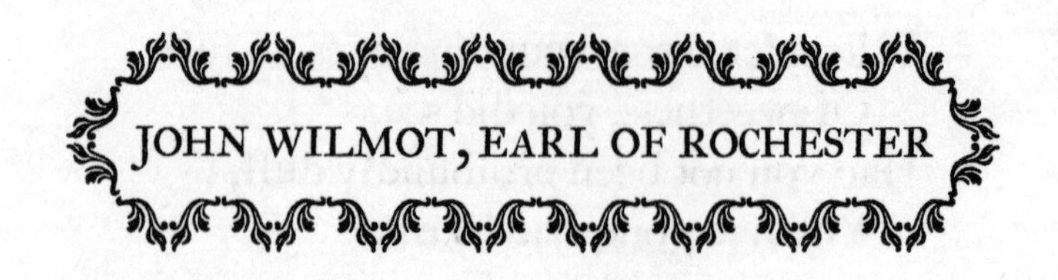

JOHN WILMOT, EARL OF ROCHESTER

58. *Love and Life*

ALL my past life is mine no more;
　The flying hours are gone:
Like transitory dreams giv'n o'er,
Whose images are kept in store
　By memory alone.

Whatever is to come, is not;
　How can it then be mine?
The present moment 's all my lot;
And that, as fast as it is got,
　PHILLIS, is wholly thine.

Then talk not of inconstancy,
　False hearts, and broken vows;
If I, by miracle, can be
This live-long minute true to thee,
　'Tis all that Heav'n allows.

59. *Cornelius Gallus Imitated*

My goddess, Lydia, heav'nly fair!
As lillys sweet, as soft as air,
Let loose thy tresses, spread thy charms,
And to my love give fresh alarms.

O! let me gaze on those bright eyes,
Tho' sacred lightning from 'em flies:
Shew me that soft, that modest grace,
Which paints with charming red thy face.

Give me ambrosia in a kiss,
That I may rival Jove in bliss;
That I may mix my soul with thine
And make the pleasure all divine.

O! hide thy bosom's killing white
(The Milky-Way is not so bright),
Lest you my ravish'd soul oppress
With beauty's pomp and sweet excess.

Why draw'st thou from the purple flood
Of my kind heart the vital blood?
Thou are all over endless charms;
O! take me, dying, to thy arms.

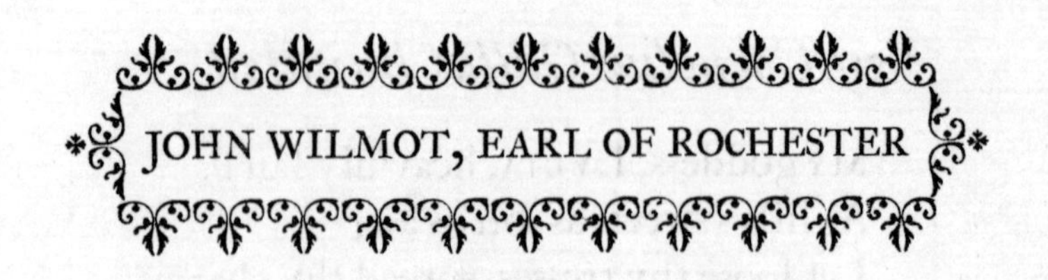

JOHN WILMOT, EARL OF ROCHESTER

60

My dear Mistris has a heart
  Soft as those kind looks she gave me;
When, with love's resistless art,
  And her eyes, she did inslave me.
But her constancy 's so weak,
  She 's so wild, and apt to wander,
That my jealous heart wou'd break,
  Should we live one day asunder.

Melting joys about her move,
  Killing pleasures, wounding blisses;
She can dress her eyes in love,
  And her lips can arm with kisses.
Angels listen when she speaks,
  She 's my delight, all mankind's wonder:
But my jealous heart would break,
  Should we live one day asunder.

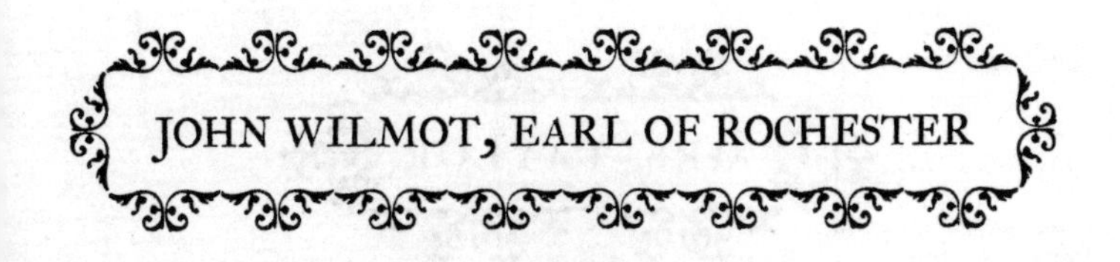

JOHN WILMOT, EARL OF ROCHESTER

61

I PROMIS'D SYLVIA to be true;
Nay, out of zeal, I swore it too:
And, that she might believe me more,
Gave her in writing what I swore:
Not vows, not oaths, can lovers bind;
So long as bless'd, so long they're kind:
'Twas in a leaf; the wind but blew:
Away both leaf and promise flew.

MRS. TAYLOR

62

STREPHON has fashion, wit and youth,
   With all things else that please;
He nothing wants but love and truth,
   To ruine me with ease:
But he is flint, and bears the art
   To kindle strong desire;
His pow'r inflames another's heart,
   Yet he ne're feels the fire.

Alas! it does my soul perplex,
   When I his charms recall,
To think he should despise the sex,
   Or what 's worse, love 'em all:
My wearied heart, like NOAH's dove,
   In vain may seek for rest;
Finding no hope to fix my love,
   Returns into my breast.

PHILIP AYRES

63. *The Request. To Love*

O LOVE, who in my breast's most noble part
Did'st that fair image lodge, that form divine,
In whom the summ of heavenly graces shine,
And there ingrav'dst it with thy golden dart:

Now, mighty work man! help me by thy art
(Since my dull pen trembles to strike a line)
That I on paper copy the design,
By thee express'd so lively in my heart.

Lend me, when I this great attempt do try,
A feather from thy wings, that, whilst to write
My hand's imploy'd, my thoughts may soar on high;
Thy torch, which fires our hearts and burns so bright,
My darker fancy let its flame supply,
And through my numbers dart celestial light.

PHILIP AYRES

64. *Love's Contrariety*

I MAKE no war, and yet no peace have found;
With heat I melt, when starv'd to death with cold:
I soar to heav'n, while groveling on the ground,
Embrace the world, yet nothing do I hold.

I'm not confin'd, yet cannot I depart,
Nor loose the chain, tho' not a captive led;
Love kills me not, yet wounds me to the heart,
Will neither have m'alive, nor have me dead.

Being blind, I see; not having voice, I cry;
I wish for death, while I of life make choice;
I hate my self, yet love you tenderly;
Do feed of tears, and in my grief rejoice.

Thus, CYNTHIA, all my health is but disease;
Both life and death do equally displease.

65. The Restless Lover

THE birds to wanton in the air desire;
The salamander sports himself in fire;
The fish in water plays; and of the earth
Man ever takes possession at his birth:
Only unhappy I, who, born to grieve,
In all these elements at once do live:
Grief does with air of sighs my mouth supply;
My wretched body on cold earth does lye;
The streams which from mine eyes flow, night
 and day,
Cannot the fire which burns my heart allay.

66. *Cynthia Sporting*

ALONG the river's side did CYNTHIA stray,
More like a goddess than a nymph at play;
The flood stopt to behold her; pleas'd to see't,
She to its kisses yields her naked feet.

Brisk air saluted her, ne'er stay'd to wooe;
The very boughs reach'd to be toying, too;
The little birds came thronging to admire,
And for her entertainment made a choire.

The meadows smile, and joy surrounds the place,
As if all things were infl'enc'd by her face;
The grass and leaves take freshness from her eyes,
And, as of lesser force, SOL's beams despise.

No herb, press'd by her foot, but blossomes strait;
Flowers, for her touch to ripen them, do wait;
They, from her hand, new fragrancy do yield;
Her presence fills with perfumes all the field.

67

ONLY tell her that I love;
  Leave the rest to her and Fate;
Some kind planet from above
May perhaps her pity move:
  Lovers on their stars must wait;
Only tell her that I love.

Why, oh why, should I despair?
  Mercy's pictur'd in her eye;
If she once vouchsafe to hear,
Welcome hope, and farewel fear:
  She's too good to let me dye;
Why, oh why, should I despair?

JOHN, BARON CUTTS

68. *Farewell to Phillis*

One look, and I am gone;
  Phillis, my part is done;
Death your pale rival's come,
  And calls me home:
Clasp'd in her frozen arms,
I shall be free from harms,
  And only pity thee
  In misery;
For, since your kindness is turn'd into
  hate,
From cruel you I'le fly to kinder Fate:
  Then, too late,
You'l wish me back again;
  Then, too late,
You'l pity him your eyes have slain.

JOHN SHEFFIELD, DUKE OF BUCKINGHAMSHIRE

69

COME, CÆLIA, let's agree at last
  To love and live in quiet;
And tie the knot so very fast
  That time shall ne're untie it.

Love's purest joys they never prove
  Who free from quarrels live;
'Tis sure the tender'st part of love
  Each other to forgive.

When first I seem'd concern'd I took
  No pleasure nor no rest;
And, when I shew'd an angry look,
  Alas! I lov'd you best.

Say but the same to me, you'l find
  How happy is our fate.
Ah! to be grateful, to be kind,
  It never is too late.

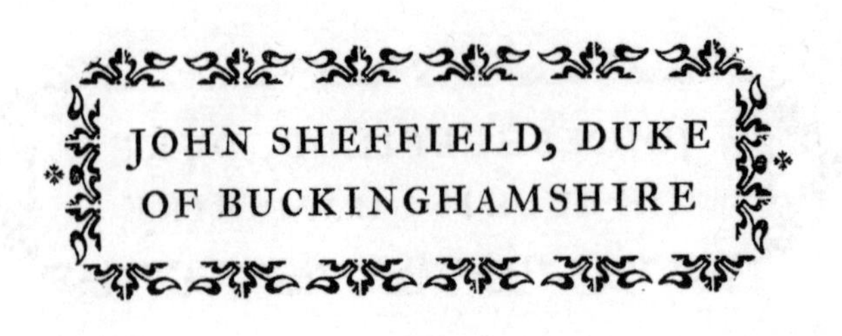

JOHN SHEFFIELD, DUKE OF BUCKINGHAMSHIRE

70

FROM all uneasie passions free,
Revenge, ambition, jealousie,
Contented, I had been too blest,
If love and you would let me rest:
Yet that dull life I now despise;
  Safe from your eyes,
I fear'd no griefs, but Oh! I found no joys.

Amidst a thousand soft desires,
Which beauty moves and love inspires,
I feel such pangs of jealous fear,
No heart so kind as mine can bear:
Yet I'll defie the worst of harms;
  Such are those charms,
'Tis worth a life to die within your arms.

WILLIAM MOUNTFORT

71

Lucinda, close or veil your eye,
Where thousand loves in ambush lye,
Where darts are pointed with such skill
They're sure to hurt, if not to kill:
Let pity move thee to seem blind,
Lest, seeing, thou destroy mankind.

Lucinda, hide that swelling breast;
The Phoenix else will change her nest:
Yet do not, for, when she expires,
Her heat may light in the soft fires
Of love and pity, so that I
By this one way may thee enjoy.

72. *To Cælia desiring his Absence*

YES, now you have your wish, but Ah! be kind
To the poor captive heart I leave behind;
For, though I go, yet that with thee remains,
Proud that 'tis thine, and triumphs in its chains.
For all the beauties that are now unblown,
When in their gaudiest prime they shall be shown,
And kneeling to be lov'd, I'de not my flame disown;
Though by that time perhaps thy charms might wast,
And the gay bloom of smiling youth be past.
Yet you inflexible, obdurate prove,
And cry, *'Tis false, 'tis feign'd, not real love:*
O cease those thoughts, and cease to be severe;
For by thy self, thy awful self, I swear,
I love too well, and must with grief confess,
Those men much happier that can love thee less

73. *The Result of Loving*

CÆLIA is cruel; SILVIA, thou,
  I must confess, art kind;
But in her cruelty, I vow,
  I more repose can find:
For O thy fancy at all game does fly,
Fond of address, and willing to comply.

Thus he that loves must be undone;
  Each way on rocks we fall:
Either you will be kind to none,
  Or worse, be kind to all.
Vain are our hopes, and endless is our care;
We must be jealous, or we must despair.

ANONYMOUS

74

FAIR SYLVIA, cease to blame my youth
For having lov'd before;
So men, till they have learnt the truth,
Strange deities adore:
My heart, 'tis true, has often rang'd
Like bees o'er gaudy flow'rs,
And many thousand loves has chang'd,
Till it was fix'd on yours.

But, SYLVIA, when I saw those eyes,
'Twas soon determin'd there;
Stars might as well forsake the skies,
And vanish in despair:
When I from this great rule do err,
New beauties to implore,
May I again turn wanderer,
And never settle more.

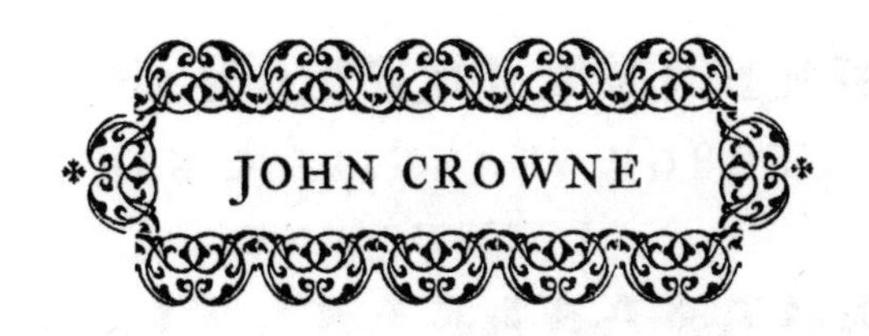

JOHN CROWNE

75

I ONCE had virtue, wealth and fame;
Now I'm a ruin'd sinner:
I lost 'em all at love's sweet game,
Yet think myself a winner.

Since that dear lovely youth to gain
My heart was long pursuing,
I'm rich enough, nor shall complain
Of such a sweet undoing.

I'le laugh at cruell fortune's spight,
While I have any feature
To keep his love, for that 's delight
Enough for mortall creature.

The sport 's so pleasant, you will own,
When once you have been in it,
You'd gladly be an age undone,
For one such charming minute.

GEORGE GRANVILLE, BARON LANSDOWNE

76. *To Mira*

THOUGHTFUL nights, and restless waking,
   Oh, the pains that we endure!
Broken faith, unkind forsaking,
   Ever doubting, never sure.

Hopes deceiving, vain endeavours,
   What a race has love to run!
False protesting, fleeting favours,
   Ev'ry, ev'ry way undone.

Still complaining and defending,
   Both to love, yet not agree,
Fears tormenting, passion rending,
   O the pangs of jealousy!

From such painful ways of living,
   Ah! how sweet, cou'd love be free;
Still presenting, still receiving,
   Fierce, immortal extasy.

77. *Song to Mira*

WHY should a heart so tender break?
    O MIRA! give its anguish ease;
The use of beauty you mistake,
    Not meant to vex, but please.

Those lips for smiling were design'd;
    That bosom to be prest;
Your eyes to languish and look kind;
    For amorous arms, your waist.

Each thing has its appointed right,
    Establish'd by the pow'rs above;
The sun to give us warmth and light,
    MIRA to kindle love.

78. *Love*

LOVE is begot by fancy, bred
    By ignorance, by expectation fed,
Destroy'd by knowledge, and, at best,
Lost in the moment 'tis possest.

79. *To Flavia. Written on her Garden in the North, &c.*

WHAT charm is this, that in the midst of snow,
 Of storms and blasts, the choicest fruits do grow?
Melons on beds of ice are taught to bear,
And, strangers to the sun, yet ripen here;
On frozen ground the sweetest flow'rs arise,
Unseen by any light but FLAVIA's eyes;
Where-e'er she treads, beneath the charmer's feet,
The rose, the jess'min, and the lillies meet;
Where-e'er she looks, behold some sudden birth
Adorns the trees, and fructifies the earth;
In midst of mountains and unfruitful ground
As rich an EDEN as the first is found.
In this new paradise the goddess reigns
In sovereign state, and mocks the lover's pains.
Beneath those beams that scorch us from her eyes,
Her snowy bosom still unmelted lies.
Love from her lips spreads all his odours round,
But bears on ice, and springs from frozen ground.
 So cold the clime that can such wonders bear,
 The garden seems an emblem of the fair.

80. *Mira: At a Review of the Guards in Hyde-Park*

LET meaner beauties conquer singly still,
But haughty MIRA will by thousands kill;
Thro' armèd ranks triumphantly she drives,
And with one glance commands a thousand lives:
The trembling heroes nor resist nor fly,
But at the head of all their squadrons die.

81

THE happiest mortals once were we;
I lov'd MIRA, MIRA me:
Each desirous of the blessing,
Nothing wanting but possessing,
I lov'd MIRA, MIRA me;
The happiest mortals once were we.

But since cruel fates dissever,
Torn from love, and torn for ever,
Tortures end me,
Death befriend me!
Of all pains, the greatest pain
Is to love, and love in vain.

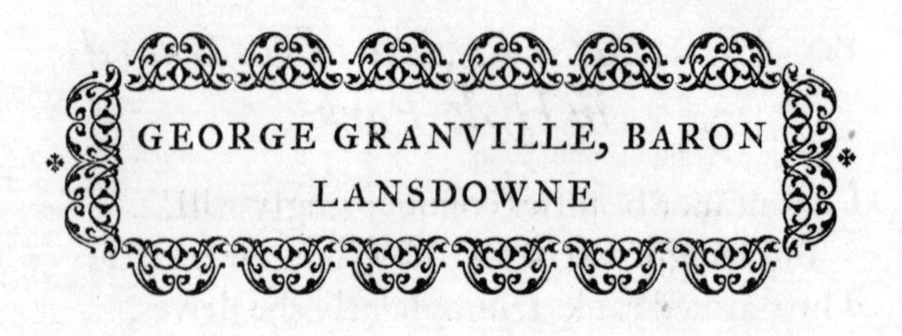

GEORGE GRANVILLE, BARON LANSDOWNE

82. *Song to Mira*

Why, cruel creature, why so bent
  To vex a tender heart?
To gold and title you relent;
  Love throws in vain his dart.

Let glittering fools in Courts be great;
  For pay, let armies move;
Beauty should have no other bait
  But gentle vows and love.

If on those endless charms you lay
  The value that's their due,
Kings are themselves too poor to pay,
  A thousand worlds to few.

But, if a passion without vice,
  Without disguise or art,
Ah Mira! if true love's your price,
  Behold it in my heart.

83. *Cloe*

CLOE's the wonder of her sex;
'Tis well her heart is tender:
How might such killing eyes perplex,
With virtue to defend her!

But nature, graciously inclin'd,
With lib'ral hand to please us,
Has to her boundless beauty join'd
A boundless bent to ease us.

84. *Adieu L'Amour*

HERE end my chains, and thraldom cease,
If not in joy, I'll live in peace:
Since, for the pleasures of an hour,
We must endure an age of pain,
I'll be this abject thing no more;
Love, give me back my heart again.

Despair tormented first my breast;
Now falshood, a more cruel guest:
O! for the peace of human-kind,
Make women longer true, or sooner kind;
With justice, or with mercy, reign,
O love! or give me back my heart again.

85

LOVE 's a dream of mighty treasure,
  Which in fancy we possess;
In the folly lies the pleasure,
  Wisdom ever makes it less.
When we think, by passion heated,
  We a goddess have in chase,
IXION-like we all are cheated,
  And a gaudy cloud embrace.

Only happy is the lover,
  Whom his mistress well deceives;
Seeking nothing to discover,
  He contented lives at ease.
But the wretch that will be knowing
  What the fair one would disguise,
Labours for his own undoing,
  Changing happy, to be wise.

86

WHAT shall I do to show how much I love her?
How many millions of sighs can suffice?
That which wins other hearts never can move her;
Those common methods of love she'll despise.

I will love more than man 'ere lov'd before me,
Gaze on her all the day, melt all the night,
Till for her own sake at last she'll implore me
To love her less to preserve our delight.

Since Gods themselves could not ever be loving,
Men must have breathing recruits for new joys:
I wish my love could be always improving,
Tho' eager love more than sorrow destroys.

IN fair AURELIA's arms leave me expiring,
To be embalm'd by the sweets of her breath;
To the last moment I'll still be desiring:
Never had hero so glorious a death.

87. *Dorinda Weeping*

STAY, pretty prodigal, oh stay;
Throw not those pearly drops away;
Each little shining gem might be
Price for a captive prince's liberty:
See down her cheeks the shining jewels slide,
Brighter than meteors that from heaven do glide.

Sorrow n'ere look'd before so fair,
Nor ever had so sweet an air:
All-conquering rays her woes do dart,
And unknown passions to the soul impart:
More fair she looks, while grief her face doth
shrowd,
Than the sun peeping thro' a wat'ry cloud.

Oh, turn away those killing eyes!
VENUS from such a sea did rise:
Love doth in tears triumphant ride;
Such mighty charms can never be deni'd:
That at one sight such different passions move,
Relenting pitty, and commanding love.

Come, curious artist, as they fall,
Gather the shining jewels all;
Harden the gems, and each will be
More valued than the INDIES' treasury:
But, if the secret doth exceed thy art,
It is but borrowing hardness from her heart.

HENRY CROMWELL

88

No, no, I ne'r shall love thee less,
For all thy fierce disdain;
So fast thy blooming charms increase,
Thy sparkling eyes my heart oppress,
Each glance renews my pain.

Yet must I (Fate!), like busie flies,
Still to thy brightness turn;
Pursue thee with my restless eyes,
Till, as each flaming blush does rise,
Insensibly I burn.

89

Written in the Leaves of a Fan

FLAVIA the least and slightest toy
Can with resistless art employ:
This fan, in meaner hands, wou'd prove
An engine of small force in love;
Yet she, with graceful air and meen
(Not to be told, or safely seen),
Directs its wanton motions so
That it wounds more than CUPID's bow:
Gives coolness to the matchless dame,
To every other breast a flame.

90

How hardly I conceal'd my tears!
   How oft did I complain!
When many tedious days my fears
   Told me I lov'd in vain.

But now my joys as wild are grown,
   And hard to be conceal'd,
Sorrow may make a silent moan,
   But joy will be reveal'd.

I tell it to the bleating flocks,
   To every stream and tree,
And bless the hollow murmuring rocks
   For ecchoing back to me.

Thus you may see with how much joy
   We want, we wish, believe:
'Tis hard such passion to destroy
   But easie to deceive.

91. *A Short Visit*

So the long absent winter-sun,
  When of the cold we most complain,
Comes slow, but swift away does run;
  Just shews the day, and sets again.

So the prime beauty of the spring,
  The virgin lilly, works our eyes;
No sooner blown, but the gay thing
  Steals from th' admirer's sight, and dyes.

The gaudy sweets o'th' infant year,
  That ravish both the smell and view,
Do thus deceitfully appear,
  And fade as soon as smelt unto.

AMINTA, tho' she be more fair
  Than untoucht lillys, chast as those,
Welcome as suns in winter are,
  And sweeter than the blowing rose,

Yet when she brought, as late she did,
  All that a dying heart cou'd ease,
And by her swift return forbid
  The joys to last, she 's too like these.

Ah tyrant beauty! do you thus
  Increase our joy to make it less?
And do you only shew to us
  A heav'n, without design to bless?

This was unmercifully kind,
  And all our bliss too dear has cost:
For is it not a hell to find
  We had a paradise that 's lost?

92

PRETHEE, CLOE, not so fast:
Let's not run and wed in hast;
We've a thousand things to do;
You must fly, and I persue,
You must frown, and I must sigh,
I intreat, and you deny.
Stay—If I am never crost,
Half the pleasure will be lost;
Be, or seem to be, severe;
Give me reason to despair;
Fondness will my wishes cloy,
Make me careless of the joy.
Lovers may, of course, complain
Of their trouble and their pain;
But, if pain and trouble cease,
Love without it will not please.

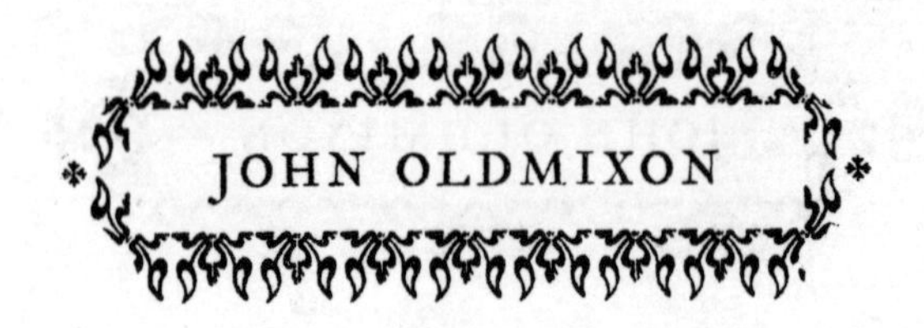

93

THOSE arts which common beauties move,
  CORINNA, you despise:
You think there 's nothing wise in love,
  Or eloquent in sighs.
You laugh at ogle, cant, and song,
  And promises abuse:
But say—for I have courted long—
  What methods shall I use?

We must not praise your charms and wit,
  Nor talk of dart and flame;
But sometimes you can think it fit
  To smile at what you blame.
Your sex's forms, which you disown,
  Alas! you can't forbear;
But in a minute smile and frown,
  Are tender and severe.

Corinna, let us now be free;
No more your arts pursue,
Unless you suffer me to be
As whimsical as you.
At last the vain dispute desist,
To love resign the field:
'Twas custom forced you to resist,
And custom bids you yield.

94

I lately vow'd, but 'twas in hast,
That I no more wou'd court
The joys which seem, when they are past,
As dull as they are short.
I oft to hate my mistress swear,
But soon my weakness find;
I make my oaths when she 's severe,
And break 'em when she 's kind.

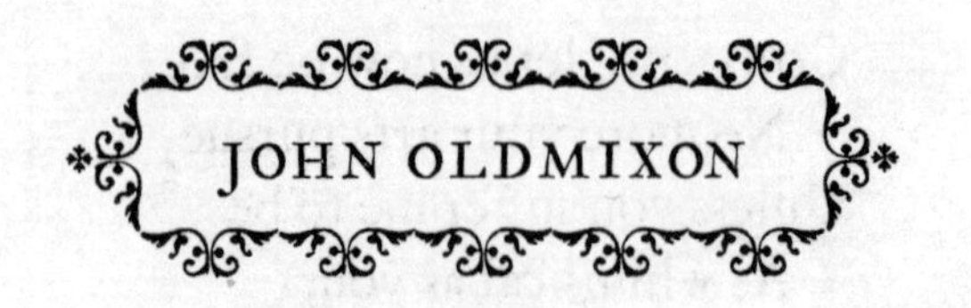

95

Fye, Cœlia, scorn the little arts
Which meaner beauties use,
Who think they can't secure our hearts
Unless they still refuse;
Are coy and shy, will seem to frown,
To raise our passions higher;
But when the poor deceit is known,
It quickly palls desire.

Come, let's not trifle time away,
Or stop you know not why;
Your blushes and your eyes betray
What death you mean to die:
Let all your maiden fears be gone,
And love no more be crost;
Ah, Cœlia, when the joys are known,
You'll curse the minutes lost.

96

To His Mistress: Against Marriage

YES, all the world must sure agree,
He who's secur'd of having thee
  Will be entirely blest:
But 'twere in me too great a wrong
To make one who have been so long
  My Queen, my slave at last.

Nor ought those things to be confin'd,
That were for public good design'd;
  Cou'd we, in foolish pride,
Make the sun always with us stay,
'Twou'd burn our corn and grass away,
  To starve the world beside.

Let not the thoughts of parting fright
Two souls which passion does unite;
  For, while our love does last,
Neither will strive to go away;
And why the devil shou'd we stay,
  When once that love is past?

97. *Upon a Favour Offer'd*

CÆLIA, too late you wou'd repent:
The off'ring all your store
Is now but like a pardon sent
To one that 's dead before.

When at the first you cruel prov'd,
And grant the bliss too late,
You hinder'd me of one I lov'd,
To give me one I hate.

I thought you innocent as fair,
When first my court I made;
But, when your falshoods plain appear,
My love no longer stay'd.

Your bounty of those favours shown,
Whose worth you first deface,
Is melting valu'd medals down
And giving us the brass.

Oh! since the thing we beg 's a toy,
That 's priz'd by love alone,
Why cannot women grant the joy
Before our love is gone?

98. *Lyce*

GO, said old LYCE, senceless lover, go,
And with soft verses court the fair; but know,
With all thy verses thou cans't get no more
Than fools without one verse have had before.
Enrag'd at this, upon the bawd I flew;
And that which most enrag'd me was, 'twas true.

99

I GENTLY touch'd her hand: she gave
A look that did my soul enslave;
I prest her rebel lips in vain:
They rose up to be prest again.
  Thus happy, I no farther meant,
  Than to be pleas'd and innocent.

On her soft breasts my hand I laid,
And a quick, light impression made;
They with a kindly warmth did glow,
And swell'd, and seem'd to over-flow.
  Yet, trust me, I no farther meant,
  Than to be pleas'd and innocent.

On her eyes my eyes did stay:
O'er her smooth limbs my hands did stray;
Each sense was ravish'd with delight,
And my soul stood prepar'd for flight.
  Blame me not if at last I meant
  More to be pleas'd than innocent.

GEORGE FARQUHAR

100

How bless'd are lovers in disguise!
   Like gods they see,
   As I do thee,
Unseen by human eyes:
   Expos'd to view,
   I'm hid from you;
I'm alter'd, yet the same:
   The dark conceals me;
   Love reveals me,
Love, which lights me by its flame.

Were you not false, you me would know;
   For, tho' your eyes
   Cou'd not devise,
Your heart had told you so:
   Your heart wou'd beat
   With eager heat,
And me by sympathy would find:
   True love might see
   One chang'd like me;
False love is only blind.

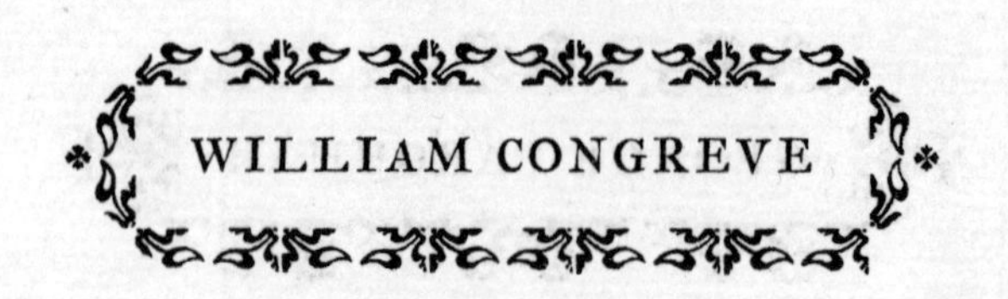

WILLIAM CONGREVE

101

LOVE's but the frailty of the mind,
When 'tis not with ambition join'd;
A sickly flame, which if not fed expires,
And feeding, wasts in self-consuming fires.

'Tis not to wound a wanton boy
Or am'rous youth, that gives the joy;
But 'tis the glory to have pierc'd a swain
For whom inferiour beauties sigh'd in vain.

Then I alone the conquest prize,
When I insult a rival's eyes:
If there's delight in love, 'tis when I see
That heart which others bleed for, bleed for me.

102

PIOUS CELINDA goes to pray'rs,
If I but ask the favour;
And yet the tender fool 's in tears
When she believes I'le leave her.

Wou'd I were free from this restraint,
Or else had hopes to win her;
Wou'd she cou'd make of me a saint,
Or I of her a sinner.

103

SEE, see, she wakes, SABINA wakes!
And now the sun begins to rise:
Less glorious is the morn that breaks
From his bright beams, than her fair eyes.

With light united, day they give,
But diff'rent fates e'er night fulfil:
How many by his warmth will live!
How many will her coldness kill!

WILLIAM CONGREVE

104

FALSE though she be to me and love,
  I'll ne'er pursue revenge;
For still the charmer I approve,
  Tho' I deplore her change.

In hours of bliss we oft have met;
  They could not always last:
And though the present I regret,
  I'm grateful for the past.

ELIJAH FENTON

105. *The Rose*

SEE, SYLVIA, see this new-blown rose!
The image of thy blush,
Mark how it smiles upon the bush,
And triumphs as it grows.
Oh pluck it not! we'll come anon;
Thou say'st: Alas! 'twill then be gone.
Now its purple beauty's spread,
Soon it will drop and fall,
And soon it will not be at all;
No fine things draw a length of thread:
Then tell me, seems it not to say,
Come on, and crop me whilst you may?

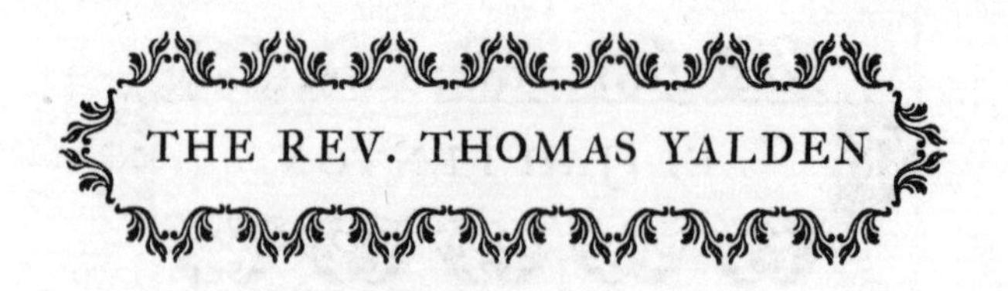

THE REV. THOMAS YALDEN

106. *Advice to a Lover*

For many unsuccessful years
At Cynthia's feet I lay;
Batt'ring them often with my tears,
I sigh'd, but durst not pray.
No prostrate wretch before the shrine
Of some lov'd saint above
Ere thought his goddess more divine
Or paid more awful love.

Still the disdainful nymph look'd down
With coy insulting pride,
Receiv'd my passion with a frown,
Or turn'd her head aside.
Then Cupid whisper'd in my ear:
Use more prevailing charms;
You modest whining fool, draw near,
And clasp her in your arms.

With eager kisses tempt the maid;
From C*YNTHIA's feet depart;*
The lips he briskly must invade
That wou'd possess the heart.
With that I shook off all the slave,
My better fortunes try'd;
When CYNTHIA in a moment gave
What she for years denied.

107

Fly, fly, you happy shepherds, fly;
  Avoid Philira's charms;
The rigour of her heart denies
  The heaven that's in her arms:
Ne'er hope to gaze and then retire,
  Nor yielding, to be blest;
Nature, who form'd her eyes of fire,
  Of ice compos'd her breast.

Yet, lovely maid, this once believe
  A slave whose zeal you move:
The gods, alas! your youth deceive;
  Their heaven consists in love:
In spight of all the thanks you owe,
  You may reproach 'em this,
That where they did their form bestow
  They have deny'd their bliss.

MATTHEW PRIOR

108. *Cupid Mistaken*

As after noon one summer's day
  Venus stood bathing in a river,
Cupid a-shooting went that way,
  New strung his bow, new fill'd his quiver.

With skill he chose his sharpest dart,
  With all his might his bow he drew;
Aim'd at his beauteous parent's heart,
  With certain speed the arrow flew.

I faint! I die! the goddess cry'd:
  O cruel, could'st thou find none other
To wreck thy spleen on? Parricide!
  Like Nero *thou hast slain thy mother.*

Poor Cupid, sobbing, scarce could speak:
  Indeed, Mamma, I did not know ye.
Alas! how easie my mistake!
  I took you for your likeness, Cloe.

109. *To Cloe, Weeping*

SEE, whilst thou weep'st, fair CLOE, see
The world in sympathy with thee.
The chearful birds no longer sing,
But drop the head, and hang the wing.
The clouds have bent their bosom lower,
And shed their sorrows in a show'r.
The brooks beyond their limits flow,
And louder murmurs speak their woe.
The nymphs and swains adopt thy cares;
They heave thy sighs, and weep thy tears.
Fantastick nymph! that grief should move
The heart obdurate against love.
Strange tears! whose pow'r can soften all
But that dear breast on which they fall.

110. *The Enchantment*

I DID but look and love awhile;
  'Twas but for one half hour:
Then to resist I had no will,
  And now I have no power.

To sigh and wish is all my ease,
  Sighs which do heat impart,
Enough to melt the coldest ice,
  Yet cannot warm your heart.

O! would your pity give my heart
  One corner of your breast;
'Twould learn of yours the winning art,
  And quickly steal the rest.

III. *The Enjoyment*

CLASP'D in the arms of her I love,
In vain, alas! for life I strove;
My flutt'ring spirits, wrap'd in fire
 By love's mysterious art,
Born on the wings of fierce desire,
 Flew from my flaming heart.

Thus lying in a trance for dead,
Her swelling breasts bore up my head,
When, waking from a pleasing dream,
 I saw her killing eyes,
Which did in fiery glances seem
 To say, *Now Cælia dies.*

Fainting, she press'd me in her arms,
And trembling lay, dissolv'd in charms,
When with a shivering voice she cry'd,
 Must I alone then die?
No, no, I languishing reply'd,
 I'll bear thee company.

Melting our souls thus into one,
Swift joys our wishes did out-run;
Then, launch'd in rolling seas of bliss,
We bid the world *adieu*,
Swearing by every charming kiss
To be for ever true.

112

I SAW LUCINDA's bosom bare;
  Transparent was the skin;
As thro' a crystal did appear
  A beating heart within.

The beating heart transfix'd I saw,
  And yet the heart was stone;
I saw it bleed, and by the wound
  I thought it was mine own.

But O! when I perceiv'd it was
  Enshrin'd within your breast,
I knew 'twas yours, for mine, alas!
  Was never yet so blest.

113. *The Roses*

Go, lovely pair of roses, go,
  This clad in scarlet, that in snow.
Go, say to my ungentle fair,
  (If on your forms she deigns to gaze)
You dare not hope to rival her,
  Or match the glories of her face;
But that you're humbly sent to prove
A youth undone by beauty and her love.

  The sickly white in this pale rose
  My wan and meager looks disclose;
  But that which shines so fiercely bright,
    Whose head in painted flames aspires,
  And blushes so with purple light,
    It seems to send forth real fires,
Tell her that rose's ruddy fires impart
The flames her eyes have kindled in my heart.

114. *The Fashionable Lover*

Love's the fever of the mind;
'Tis a grief that none can cure,
Till the nymph you love prove kind;
She can give you ease again;
She can best remove the pain
Which you for her endure.

Be not ever then repining,
Sighing, dying, canting, whining;
Spend not time in vain pursuing;
If she does not love you, make her;
When she loves you, then—forsake her;
'Tis the modish way of wooing.

115. *Love's a Riddle*

THE flame of love asswages
  When once it is reveal'd;
But fiercer still it rages,
  The more it is conceal'd.

Consenting makes it colder;
  When met it will retreat:
Repulses make it bolder,
  And dangers make it sweet.

NOTES ON THE SOURCES

THE first title given in each of the following notes is the title of the book in which the song in question was first printed. The text is taken from this source unless I have expressly stated otherwise. I have also attempted, for the guidance of students and musicians, to indicate contemporary volumes in which the songs were reprinted. I cannot hope to have traced every printing of every song; but the lists given will provide some indication of the relative popularity of the songs in their time.

For bibliographical guidance I have quoted, wherever relevant, the reference number of each book in the following three bibliographies: *English Song-Books, 1651–1702*, by Cyrus Lawrence Day and Eleanore Boswell Murrie (Bibliographical Society, 1940), referred to in these notes as 'D. & M.'; *A Bibliography of English Poetical Miscellanies, 1521–1750*, by Arthur E. Case (Bibliographical Society, 1935), referred to here as 'Case'; and *English Poetry: A Catalogue of . . . Works of the English Poets exhibited by the National Book League, 1947*, by John Hayward (Cambridge, illustrated edition, 1950), referred to here as 'Hayward'.

The songs have all been transcribed from the original sources. I have followed the original spelling and made no textual alterations except for the occasional correction of an obvious printer's error. I have not, however, followed the original punctuation or the use of capitals and italics.

ALEXANDER BROME (*1620–66*)

1. *Songs, and Other Poems* . . . *1661*. Although Brome really belongs to the age of Suckling and Carew, his collected songs were not published until the Restoration, and their popularity continued far into the eighteenth century. Indeed, the song I have chosen, in preference to the more familiar 'Tell me not of a face that's fair', has enjoyed a remarkable success in our own times, as sung by Mr. Elton Hayes in Mr. John Clements's production of Farquhar's *The Beaux-Stratagem*.

SIR WILLIAM DAVENANT (1606–68)

2. *The Rivals: A Comedy* . . . 1668. This song, sung by Theocles in Act III of the play, is one of the most engaging variants on a theme which recurs throughout the lyric verse of the Restoration. Davenant's last line has a tenderness of sentiment all too rare in its kind. The song was included in *New Ayres and Dialogues*, 1678 (D. & M. 46).

SIR GEORGE ETHEREGE (? 1635–91)

3. *The Comical Revenge, or, Love in a Tub* . . . 1664. Sung by Letitia in Act V, Scene iii.

4. *Catch that Catch can: or, The Musical Companion* . . . 1667 (D. & M. 26). This is the earliest version of the song which is famous in its shorter, altered version, beginning 'It is not, Celia, in our power'. It was originally set to music by Matthew Locke, whose setting was also printed in *Synopsis of Vocal Musick*, 1680 (D. & M. 53). The four-stanza version was printed in *The New Academy of Complements*, 1671 (Case 148). The more familiar version, addressed to 'Celia' and omitting the second and fourth stanzas, first appeared anonymously in *A Collection of Poems, Written upon Several Occasions, By Several Persons*, 1672 (Case 151). A musical setting of it, by 'A Person of Quality', was printed in *A Collection of New Songs*, 1696 (D. & M. 143).

5. *Westminster Drollery, The Second Part* . . . 1672. Also in *New Court-Songs, and Poems*, 1672, and *A Collection of Poems Written upon Several Occasions by Several Persons*, 1673 (Case 151 *b*). In all these miscellanies it appears anonymously. It was set to music by Thomas Stafford in *Choice Songs and Ayres*, 1673 (D. & M. 35), and *Choice Ayres, Songs and Dialogues*, 1675 (D. & M. 40), and by John Church in *Twelve New Songs . . . Figur'd for the Organ, Harpsichord, or Theorbo*, 1699 (D. & M. 181).

6. *A Duke and No Duke: A Farce.* By Nahum Tate . . . 1685. The song is printed at the end of the play, with a musical setting by 'Signor Baptist' (Giovanni Battista Draghi).

7. *Miscellany, Being a Collection of Poems by Several Hands* . . . 1685 (Case 177). Edited by Aphra Behn.

8. *Secret-Love, or The Maiden-Queen* . . . 1668. Sung by Asteria in Act IV, Scene ii. This beautiful lyric, the first of three songs written in this measure by Dryden, occurs in B.M. Harleian MS. 3991. It was reprinted in *The New Academy of Complements*, 1671 (Case 148), and *The True Lover's New Academy*, *c.* 1688. It is also to be found, with the addition of eight stanzas, amongst the Roxburghe Ballads in the B.M.

9. *Tyrannick Love, or, The Royal Martyr. A Tragedy* . . . 1670. Sung by Damilcar in Act IV, Scene i. Set to music by Henry Purcell in *Deliciae Musicae*, Book I, 1695 (D. & M. 131), and in *Orpheus Britannicus*, 1698 (D. & M. 166).

10. *The Spanish Fryar, or, The Double Discovery* . . . 1681. Sung by Leonora, Queen of Arragon, in Act V. Reprinted in *Wit & Drollery: Jovial Poems . . . with New Additions*, 1682 (Case 114*c*), and *The Complete Courtier: or, Cupid's Academy*, by J. Shurly, 1683 (Case 168). Musical setting by Captain Simon Pack was printed in *Wit and Mirth: or, Pills to Purge Melancholy*, vol. iv, 1706 (D. & M. 210*a*), and *Songs Compleat, Pleasant and Divertive*, vol. v, 1719 (D. & M. 235).

11. *An Evening's Love, or, The Mock Astrologer* . . . 1671. Sung by Wildblood in Act II. Set to music by Alphonso Marsh in *Choice Songs and Ayres*, 1673 (D. & M. 35) and in *Choice Ayres, Songs, and Dialogues*, 1675 (D. & M. 40).

12. *Cleomenes, The Spartan Heroe. A Tragedy* . . . 1692. Sung in Act II, Scene ii. Set to music by Henry Purcell in *Comes Amoris: or, The Companion of Love*, Book IV, 1693 (D. & M. 118), in *Joyful Cuckoldom, or, the Love of Gentlemen, and Gentlewomen* (D. & M. 133), and in *Wit and Mirth: or, Pills to Purge Melancholy*, vol. iv, 1706 (D. & M. 210*a*).

ANONYMOUS

13. *Westminster Drollery. Or, A Choice Collection of the Newest Songs & Poems both at Court and Theaters.* By a Person of Quality . . . 1671 (Case 150 (i) *a*). A slightly different version of this eloquent poem is in B.M. Harleian MS. 6910, f. 170.

14. *Westminster Drollery*... 1671 (Case 150(i) *a*). This song was attributed by Sir John Hawkins, in his *General History of Music*, 1776, to King Charles II. Mr. Ault has proved how slender this attribution is. He cites a manuscript version (B.M. Harl. MS. 3991) which is headed '1st. Song in the Masque, 1670'. It was undoubtedly well known in its day, and was reprinted in *The New Academy of Complements*, 1671 (Case 148), and *The Canting Academy, or, The Devil's Cabinet Opened*, 1673 (Case 155). It was set to music by Pelham Humphrey in Playford's *Choice Songs and Ayres*, 1673 (D. & M. 35), and later editions.

SIR CHARLES SEDLEY (?1639–1701)

15. *The Mulberry-Garden, A Comedy*... 1668. Sung by Victoria in Act III, Scene ii. This lovely lyric was one of the most popular love-songs of the century. It was reprinted in *The New Academy of Complements*, 1671 (Case 148), *Windsor Drollery*, 1671, *Wit and Drollery*, 1682 (Case 114*c*), *The Academy of Complements*, 1684, and *The Theatre of Complements*, 1688.

16–21. All these songs were first printed in *A Collection of Poems, Written upon Several Occasions, by Several Persons. London, Printed for Hobart Kemp* . . . 1672 (Hayward 122; Case 151). This collection was substantially reprinted, with additions, for Thos. Collins and John Ford in 1673, and for Francis Saunders in 1693 and 1695 (then entitled *The Temple of Death*, &c.). It was again reissued and expanded by Daniel Brown and Benjamin Tooke in 1701. In its various guises this must be considered one of the most influential anthologies of the seventeenth century. I have not, however, taken my texts of Sedley's songs from this source, but from *The Miscellaneous Works of the Honourable Sir Charles Sedley*, 1702. There are many textual differences between the versions in this, the first 'collected' edition or Sedley, and Hobart Kemp's collection of 1672. I have chosen the later versions because they are in most cases preferable on grounds of style. Also, the later versions were 'published from the original manuscripts by Capt. Ayloffe', a kinsman of Sedley's, who seems to have acted, in effect, as his literary executor. We may take it that the versions printed in 1702 in the *Miscellaneous Works* were the author's approved copies, whereas those published in 1672 may well have been obtained by Kemp at second or third hand.

16. See above. Kemp's version differed only slightly in lines 12 and 13. *Windsor Drollery*, 1671, and *Westminster Drollery*, 1671, contain a poem which resembles this, beginning

> Bright CELIA, know, 'twas not thine eyes
> Alone that did me first surprise.

17. See above. Kemp's version has a variant in line 10 and an additional couplet at the end.

18. See above. This song had two additional couplets in Kemp's version, and lines 12 and 16 were quite different. A shorter version appeared in *Westminster Drollery*, Part II, 1672 (Case 150 (2)*a*).

19. See above. Kemp's version has several variants and two additional couplets. The metaphors in line 10 refer to cards or dice playing. This song was reprinted in *The Academy of Complements*, 1684.

20. See above. Kemp's version is addressed to Hermione, not Celemene. There are slight differences in the sixth stanza and there is an additional stanza at the end. It is remarkable that this poem, the first line of which is probably Sedley's most famous line, does not appear to have been reprinted during the seventeenth century, except in the later editions of Kemp's miscellany. Nor was it set to music. (Indeed, it is worth noting that fewer of Sedley's poems were set to music than Etherege's, Dorset's, or Dryden's.)

21. See above. I have followed other editors in correcting the third word of the first line of the third stanza from 'is' to 'in'. Kemp's version has several differences, notably in the fourth line of the first stanza, which reads flatly: 'Were it my interest'. Another and less satisfactory version appeared in *Poems on Affairs of State*, 1704 (Case 211 (3)*a*). Addressed to Chloris, instead of Celia, the song was set to music by Daniel Purcell in the Third Book of Playford's *The Banquet of Musick*, 1689 (D. & M. 101).

22. *The Gentleman's Journal: or, the Monthly Miscellany*... March 1691/2. In its first publication this song had an additional stanza. It was omitted in the *Miscellaneous Works*, 1702, from which I have taken my text. The song also appeared in *The History of Adolphus ... With a Collection of Songs and Love-Verses*, 1691 (Case 196), an exceedingly rare miscellany, edited by Charles Gildon, which had not apparently been seen by Prof.

de Sola Pinto when he prepared his edition of Sedley. The song was set to music by Robert King in *A Second Booke of Songs*, *c.* 1695 (D. & M. 135).

CHARLES SACKVILLE, EARL OF DORSET (1638–1706)

23. *Westminster Drollery*... 1671 (Case 150 (i) *a*). Also in *Windsor Drollery*, 1671. Set to music by Pelham Humphrey in Playford's *Choice Songs and Ayres*, 1673 (D. & M. 35), and later editions.

24. *Choice Ayres and Songs*... 1684 (D. & M. 68), where it is set to music by Robert King. It was included also in Aphra Behn's *Miscellany*, 1685 (Case 177), where it was attributed to Rochester, and in *The Annual Miscellany*, 1694 (Case 172 (4) *a*). All three publications have textual differences. The song was attributed to Dorset in *The Works of the Most Celebrated Minor Poets*, 1749 (Case 467 (1) *a*). Mr. Ault, somewhat surprisingly, surmised that either Dorset or Rochester could have written it. I am strongly of Mr. Kerr's opinion that it is characteristic of Dorset in style and sentiment.

25. *Methinks the Poor Town has been troubled too long. Or, a Collection of all the New Songs that are generally Sung, Either at the Court or, Theatres*... 1673 (Case 156). This slim miscellany, 'collected by one of the Duke's Servants', is one of the most interesting of its period, and contains a high proportion of good verse. It takes its title from the first line of Dorset's song. The song was included in Playford's *Choice Songs and Ayres*, 1673 (D. & M. 35) and 1675 (D. & M. 40), where the setting is by John Playford himself. It also appeared in *Wit and Mirth: or, Pills to Purge Melancholy*... 1699 (D. & M. 182), and later editions. It was reprinted in the fifth part of Dryden's *Miscellany Poems*, 1704 (Case 172 (5) *a*), and in *The Works of the Earls of Rochester, Roscommon, Dorset*,.... 1721 (Case 323 (i) *a*). In the original printing blanks were left where the names of Lord Craven, the Queen, and Mr. Roper occurred in subsequent versions. I have filled them in. 'Lord Craven's drums' refers to an incident recorded by Pepys on 24 March, 1667/8, when a mob of apprentices began to pull down brothels and were dispersed by soldiers under the command of Lord Craven,

who caused an alarm to be sounded by drum and trumpet. According to A. H. Bullen, Christopher Roper was appointed page of honour to the Queen in 1667. 'Black Bess' has been identified with Mrs. Barnes.

26. *A New Miscellany of Original Poems, On Several Occasions*... 1701 (Case 223 and 223 *b*—there are two issues of this book, which was edited by Charles Gildon). Dorinda was Katherine, daughter of Sir Charles Sedley, and later Countess of Dorchester, and mistress of James II. The poem was written about 1677, and it is surprising that it did not find its way into print till 1701.

27. *The Amorous Bigotte... A Comedy. Written by Tho. Shadwell*... 1690. Sung in Act IV, Scene i. Set to music by Robert King in Playford's *The Banquet of Musick*, Book V, 1691 (D. & M. 109). It also appears in *Wit and Mirth: or, Pills to Purge Melancholy*, Part II, 1700, and later editions. In these song-books it appears anonymously. The fact that it was first sung in Shadwell's play is no proof that he was the author; it was usual for various writers to contribute songs to plays. The attribution to Dorset occurs first in *Examen Miscellaneum*, 1702 (Case 228), which was edited by Charles Gildon.

ANONYMOUS

28. *New Court-Songs, and Poems*. By R. V. Gent... 1672 (Case 153). R. V. has been identified as Robert Veal; but a number of different authors are represented in the book. Song 28 was also printed, with some variations, in *Methinks the Poor Town*... 1673 (Case 156). It was evidently popular in its time. A musical setting by Charles Forsall was printed in Playford's *Choice Songs and Ayres*, 1673 (D. & M. 35), and later editions. It also occurred in *Wit and Mirth: or, Pills to Purge Melancholy*, 1699 (D. & M. 182), and later editions, and in *Songs Compleat, Pleasant and Divertive*, vol. iii, 1719 (D. & M. 233). As in so many of the lesser songs of the period the poet changes the tenses unaccountably from line to line (just as Cloris changes her mind). I confess to have enforced some regularity of tense in the penultimate stanza.

29. *Covent Garden Drolery... The Second Impression*... 1672 (Case 152 *b*). This miscellany, edited by 'A. B.', who perhaps was

Aphra Behn, is one of the most important of its time. It was reprinted in 1927 by Montague Summers and in 1928 by G. Thorn-Drury. Song 29 also appeared in *Methinks the Poor Town...*, 1673 (Case 156), *The Theatre of Complements*, 1688, and the fifth part of Dryden's *Poetical Miscellanies*, 1704 (Case 172 (5) *a*). In *The Miscellaneous Works of . . . Rochester and Roscommon*, 1707, it was ascribed to Rochester. Mr. John Hayward included it in his edition of Rochester's *Works*, 1926, but, I understand, no longer sustains that attribution. Mr. Kerr, in his *Restoration Verse*, 1930, attributed the song to Dorset, and it certainly has the lilt and certain of the characteristic phrases of Dorset. I think, however, that more substantial evidence is required. The song was set to music by Robert Smith in Playford's *Choice Songs and Ayres*, 1673 (D. & M. 35) and later editions.

30. *Covent Garden Drolery... The Second Impression...* 1672 (Case 152 *b*). Also in *New Court-Songs*, 1672 (Case 153), *Methinks the Poor Town...*, 1673 (Case 156), and Dryden's *Poetical Miscellanies*, Part V, 1704 (Case 172 (5) *a*). Set to music by Alphonso Marsh, jr., in Playford's *Choice Songs and Ayres*, 1673 (D. & M. 35) and later editions.

31. *Covent Garden Drolery* . . . 1672 (Case 152 *a*).

32. *Covent Garden Drolery... The Second Impression*, 1672 (Case 152 *b*). Set to music by Robert Smith in *Choice Songs and Ayres*, 1673 (D. & M. 35) and later editions.

33. *Methinks the Poor Town* . . . 1673 (Case 156). Reprinted in *The Last and Best Edition of New Songs*, 1677 (Case 163).

34. *Methinks the Poor Town...* 1673 (Case 156). Also in *A Collection of Poems Written upon Several Occasions*, 1673 (Case 151 *b*). Set to music in Playford's *Choice Ayres, Songs, and Dialogues... The Second Edition*, 1675 (D. & M. 40).

35. *Methinks the Poor Town...* 1673 (Case 156). Mr. Kerr described this chorus as 'the summary and justification of all these songs'.

36. *A Collection of Poems...* 1672 (Case 151; Hayward 122). A version with a different first line appeared in *Covent Garden Drolery*, 1672 (Case 152 *a*).

APHRA BEHN (1640–89)

37. *Covent Garden Drolery*... 1672 (Case 152*a*), where it begins with the line 'I led my Silvia to a grove' and is written as though by a man. I have taken my version from Mrs. Behn's comedy, *The Dutch Lover*, 1673. It appeared also in *Methinks the Poor Town*... 1673 (Case 156). It was set by Robert Smith in Playford's *Choice Songs and Ayres*, 1673 (D. & M. 35) and later editions, and by Johann Wolfgang Franck in *Remedium Melancholiae*, 1690 (D. & M. 106).

38. *Abdelazer, or, The Moor's Revenge. A Tragedy* . . . 1677. Sung at the beginning of Act I. Also included in *The Last and Best Edition of New Songs*, 1677 (Case 163), and *The Loyal Garland*, fifth edition, 1686.

THOMAS FLATMAN (1637–88)

39. *Poems and Songs* . . . 1674.

RICHARD LEIGH (1649–1728)

40–2. *Poems, upon Several Occasions, And, to Several Persons. By the Author, of The Censure, of the Rota*... 1775. This somewhat remarkable poet has only in recent years attracted the attention that is his due. His *Poems* were reprinted by Mr. Hugh Macdonald in 1947.

THOMAS DUFFETT (*fl.* 1674–78)

43. *New Poems, Songs, Prologues and Epilogues* ... 1676. Although the *Dictionary of National Biography* describes this as 'a paltry volume', Mr. John Hayward included it in the National Book League's Exhibition of English Poetry, 1947 (No. 123). Duffett was a milliner in the New Exchange.

WILLIAM CAVENDISH, DUKE OF NEWCASTLE (1592–1676)

44. *The Humorous Lovers. A Comedy*... 1677. Sung by Boldman in Act V, Scene i. Pepys called this comedy 'the most silly thing that ever came on the stage'. The song I have quoted, however, is a superb exercise in imagery. It was probably written much earlier.

ANONYMOUS

45. *A New Collection of the Choicest Songs* . . . 1676 (Case 161). I have taken my text from *New Ayres and Dialogues*, 1678 (D. & M. 46), where it is set to music by Dr. William Turner. This setting also appeared in Playford's *Choice Ayres and Songs*, Book V, 1684 (D. & M. 68), and *Wit and Mirth: or, Pills to Purge Melancholy*, second edition, vol. iii, 1707 (D. & M. 215). The text was reprinted in *The Last and Best Edition of New Songs*, 1677 (Case 163), and *The New Help to Discourse*, third edition, 1684 (Case 141*c*).

CHARLES WEBBE (*fl.* 1678)

46. *New Ayres and Dialogues . . . By John Banister and Thomas Low* . . . 1678 (D. & M. 46). Setting by Henry Purcell. This song echoes Carew, but Webbe, as he showed in another song quoted by Ault, had a true singing note.

EPHELIA (*fl.* 1679)

47, 48. *Female Poems on Several Occasions, Written by Ephelia* . . . 1679. Sir Edmund Gosse suggested that 'Ephelia' was a daughter of Katherine Philips. She was no inconsiderable poet, and there is a real anguish in her love for the faithless 'J. G.', who jilted her, and found other consolations in Africa.

RICHARD DUKE (1658–1711)

49. *Songs set by Signior Pietro Reggio. The Second Part* . . . [1680] (D. & M. 52). Setting by Reggio. I have taken my text from Playford's *Choice Ayres and Songs*, Book IV, 1683 (D. & M. 59), where the setting is by Thomas Tudway. The song occurs in *The Compleat Courtier, or Cupid's Academy*, 1683 (Case 168), and twice in *The Newest Collection of the Choicest Songs*, 1683 (D. & M. 65). Almost all these versions have textual differences. The poem appeared as by Richard Duke in *Poems by the Earl of Roscommon . . . Together with Poems by Mr. Richard Duke*, 1717 (Case 301).

50. *The Newest Collection of the Choicest Songs*, 1683 (D. & M. 65). Also in Playford's *Choice Ayres and Songs*, Book IV, 1683 (D. & M. 59), where the setting is by Thomas Tudway. The

text, which varies in almost every version, was printed in *Examen Poeticum, Being the Third Part of Miscellany Poems*, 1693 (Case 172 (3)*a*), and in *Poems by the Earl of Roscommon*..., 1717 (Case 301). Duke was a friend of Dryden's. 'He was one of the wits,' wrote Swift, 'but turned parson and left it.' Song 50 is a decidedly unparsonical poem, but the *D.N.B.* records that Duke's 'clerical life was blameless'.

MATTHEW COPPINGER (*fl.* 1682)

51, 52. *Poems, Songs and Love-Verses*... 1682. Coppinger had an unusual talent, which has been almost entirely neglected.

THOMAS D'URFEY (1653–1723)

53. *Choice New Songs... Written by Tho. D'Urfey, Gent*... 1684 (D. & M. 69). Set to music by King.

54. *The Banquet of Musick*... Book III, 1689 (D. & M. 101). Set to music by Dr. John Blow. Also in *Songs Compleat*, vol. iii, 1719. The text was printed in D'Urfey's *New Poems*, 1690.

JOHN WILMOT, EARL OF ROCHESTER (1647–80)

The intricate textual problems of Rochester's poems are discussed by Mr. John Hayward in his edition of the *Works*, 1926. The first collected edition of Rochester's poems was published surreptitiously in 1680 (Hayward 125), purporting to have been printed in Antwerp. This edition was reprinted as 'By a late Person of Honour' in 1685. Mr. Hayward preferred Rymer's versions, as published in 1691, and reprinted in 1696 and 1705. I think there can be no final resolution of the various texts, as no collected edition was published in Rochester's lifetime and he appears to have made no effort to prepare copies for the press.

55. *Choice Ayres and Songs... The Second Book*... 1679 (D. & M. 48). Set to music by Dr. William Turner. My text is taken from *Poems on Several Occasions*, 1680, which is, except for spelling, the same as Rymer's 1691 version.

56. *Poems on Several Occasions* . . . 1691. This song was not included in the earlier editions.

57. *Poems on Several Occasions* . . . 1691. Not included in the earlier editions.

58. *Songs . . . Composed by Henry Bowman* . . . [1677] (D. & M. 44), and editions published in 1678 and 1679. Also in *Songs set by Signior Pietro Reggio*, Part II [1680] (D. & M. 52), and, set by Dr. John Blow, in Playford's *The Theater of Music*, Book I, 1685 (D. & M. 78), and in *Wit and Mirth: or, Pills to Purge Melancholy*, Part II, 1700 (D. & M. 188) and later editions. My text is from *Poems on Several Occasions*, 1680, which is the same as Rymer's, 1691.

59. *The Annual Miscellany: For the Year 1694. Being the fourth Part of Miscellany Poems* . . . 1694 (Case 172 (4) *a*).

60. *Miscellany* (edited by Aphra Behn), 1685 (Case 177). The same version was printed in Rymer's edition, 1691. The song also appeared in Bold's *Latin Songs, with their English*, 1685.

61. *Thesaurus Musicus* . . . Book V, 1696 (D. & M. 154). Set to music by Gottfried Finger. My text is taken from *Examen Miscellaneum*, 1702 (Case 228), edited by Charles Gildon. (It is, perhaps, worth recording that my copy of this miscellany has a different title-page, reading *Miscellanies in Prose and Verse* . . . 1702, printed for Nich. Cox. This is not mentioned by Case, and I have seen no other copy.)

MRS. TAYLOR (*fl.* 1685)

62. *Miscellany* . . . 1685 (Case 177), edited by Aphra Behn. This song by one of Mrs. Behn's talented ladies was reprinted, with textual variations, in *Examen Poeticum*, the Third Part of Dryden's *Miscellany Poems*, 1693 (Case 172 (3) *a*).

PHILIP AYRES (1638–1712)

63–6. *Lyric Poems, Made in Imitation of the Italians* . . . 1687 (Hayward 132). Ayres was a tutor in the family of Montagu Garrard Drake, of Amersham.

JOHN, BARON CUTTS (1661–1707)

67, 68. *Poetical Exercises, Written upon Several Occasions*... 1687. Both songs are stated in this book to have been set to music by Mr. King. I can only find the setting of Song 67, which is in *Songs for One Two and Three Voices... By R. King Servant to His Majesty*, c. 1692 (D. & M. 117). Cutts was a soldier of some distinction.

JOHN SHEFFIELD, DUKE OF BUCKINGHAMSHIRE (1648–1721)

69. *Comes Amoris*... Book I, 1687 (D. & M. 90). The setting is by Dr. William Turner. This song was reprinted in the Fifth Part of Dryden's *Miscellany Poems*, 1704 (Case 172 (5)*a*). It was not included in the 1721 edition of Sheffield's poems, but was printed in the quarto edition of 1723.

70. *A Collection of Poems by Several Hands*... 1693 (Case 151*c*). Reprinted in *The Temple of Death* . . . 1695 (Case 151*d*) and the later editions of the same collection, 1701 and 1702. Set to music in *Mercurius Musicus*, 1699 (D. & M. 174), by John Church.

WILLIAM MOUNTFORT (1664–92)

71. *The Injur'd Lovers, or, The Ambitious Father... A Tragedy*, 1688. Sung at the beginning of Act I. William Mountfort was an actor, and himself played the part of Dorenalus in the play. The song was set to music by 'Sen. Baptist' (Giovanni Battista Draghi) in Playford's *The Banquet of Musick*, Book II, 1688 (D. & M. 97), and in *Vinculum Societatis, or, The Tie of Good Company*, 1688 (D. & M. 100).

ROBERT GOULD (? 1660–? 1709)

72, 73. *Poems Chiefly Consisting of Satyrs and Satyrical Epistles*... 1689. Gould was 'nine years a servant of the Duke of Dorset', and later a schoolmaster.

ANONYMOUS

74. *The Banquet of Musick*... Book IV, 1690 (D. & M. 105). Set by Alexander Damascene. Reprinted in Fenton's *Oxford and Cambridge Miscellany Poems* [1708] (Case 248). This song was attributed to Prior in the edition of his works published in 1800. Mr. Iolo Williams conjecturally attributes it to Francis Atterbury, Bishop of Rochester.

JOHN CROWNE (*ob.* 1703)

75. *The English Frier; or, The Town Sparks. A Comedy*... 1690. Sung by Airy in Act V. Set to music by Robert King in Playford's *The Banquet of Music*, Book V, 1691 (D. & M. 109).

GEORGE GRANVILLE, BARON LANSDOWNE (1667–1735)

76. *The British Enchanters, or, No Magick like Love. A Tragedy*... 1706. Sung in Act II, Scene i. My text is taken from *The Genuine Works*, 1732.

77. *Poems upon Several Occasions*... 1712. Lord Lansdowne complained that the 1712 edition was unauthorized and printed from incorrect copies. The first edition for which he himself took responsibility was *The Genuine Works in Verse and Prose of the Right Honourable George Granville, Lord Lansdowne*, 1732. As a number of minor textual corrections were made in this edition, usually to the benefit of the verse, I have used it for most of my texts. The Mira of Lansdowne's poems is assumed to be the Countess of Newburgh, to whom he wrote verses before he was twenty-three.

78. *Poems upon Several Occasions* . . . 1712. It is to be assumed that most of Lord Lansdowne's poems were written before 1690, though no collected edition appeared until 1712.

79. *The History of Adolphus, Prince of Russia*... *With a Collection of Songs and Love-Verses. By Several Hands*... 1691 (Case 196). This curious and rare miscellany, of which the Bodleian Library possesses the only copy I have located in England, contains several of Lansdowne's verses. I have taken my text of Song 79 from *The Genuine Works*, 1732. In *The History of Adolphus* there

are several textual differences. The song also appeared in *Poems on Several Occasions*, 1712.

80. *Poems on Several Occasions* . . . 1712. Text from *The Genuine Works*, 1732.

81. *The British Enchanters* . . . 1706. Sung in Act III, Scene i. Also in *Poems* . . . 1712. Text from *The Genuine Works*, 1732.

82. *The History of Adolphus* . . . 1691 (Case 196). Here the song is addressed to Celia, not Mira. Also in *Poems* . . . 1712. Text from *The Genuine Works*, 1732.

83. *The History of Adolphus* . . . 1691 (Case 196). Also in *Poems* . . . 1712. Text from *The Genuine Works*, 1732, where it is included in *Once a Lover and Always a Lover*, a revision of a comedy called *The She-Gallants*, acted and printed in 1696. The song was set to music by Robert King in *Vinculum Societatis*, Book III, 1691 (D. & M. 110) and *A Second Booke of Songs . . . Composed by R. King*, *c.* 1695 (D. & M. 135).

84. *Poems on Several Occasions* . . . 1712. Text from *The Genuine Works*, 1732.

THOMAS CHEEKE (*fl.* 1688–1701)

85. *Vinculum Societatis, or, The Tie of Good Company* . . . Book II, 1688 (D. & M. 100). Set to music by Samuel Ackroyde. Text from *The History of Adolphus* . . . 1691 (Case 196). Reprinted, with textual variations, in Gildon's *Miscellany Poems*, 1692 (Case 197).

THOMAS BETTERTON (?1635–1710)

86. *The Prophetess: or, The History of Dioclesian* . . . 1690. This opera is an adaptation of Beaumont and Fletcher's *The Prophetess*. There is some doubt as to whether Betterton, the actor, was entirely responsible for the adaptation, and Mr. Ault was inclined to attribute this song to Dryden. Mr. Kerr dissents. Although the measure is characteristic of Dryden, and the song has real feeling and invention, it lacks the assurance and inevitability of, say, Songs 8 and 12. It was reprinted in *Wit's Cabinet*, *c.* 1700, and *The Compleat Academy of Complements*, 1705 (Case 235). Set to music by Henry Purcell in *The Vocal and*

Instrumental Musick of The Prophetess, or, The History of Dioclesian, 1691 (D. & M. 111), and in *Wit and Mirth: or, Pills to Purge Melancholy*, Part II, 1700 (D. & M. 188) and later editions, and in *Songs Compleat, Pleasant and Divertive*, vol. iv, 1719 (D. & M. 234).

THOMAS HEYRICK (1649–94)

87. *Miscellany Poems*... Cambridge, 1691 (Hayward 134). Heyrick, who was Curate of Market Harborough, was a metaphysical poet of some talent.

HENRY CROMWELL (*fl.* 1692)

88. *Miscellany Poems*, edited by Charles Gildon, 1692 (Case 197). Reprinted in *The Gentleman's Journal*, 1694, and in *The Theatre of Ingenuity*, 1704 (Case 234).

THE RT. REV. FRANCIS ATTERBURY, D.D., BISHOP OF ROCHESTER (1662–1732)

89. *The Gentleman's Journal*... 1692. Also in *Examen Poeticum: Being the Third Part of Miscellany Poems*, 1693 (Case 172 (3)*a*).

ANNE WHARTON (? 1632–85)

90. *A Collection of Poems by Several Hands*... 1693 (Case 151 *c*). Reprinted in the 1701 edition of the same anthology with a variant of the second line of the last stanza. Anne Wharton was married at the age of fourteen to Thomas Wharton, who wrote the words of 'Lillibulero', and was 'the most universal villain' Swift ever knew. Her married life was unhappy and brief.

ANONYMOUS

91. *The Annual Miscellany: For the Year 1694. Being the Fourth Part of Miscellany Poems* ... 1694 (Case 172 (4)*a*).

JOHN OLDMIXON (1673–1742)

92, 93. *Poems on Several Occasions, Written in imitation of the manner of Anacreon* . . . 1696. Song 93 is said to have been set to music by Mr. King, but I have not found the setting.

94. *Twelve New Songs* . . . 1699 (D. & M. 181). Set to music by Samuel Ackroyde. My text is taken from *Examen Miscellaneum*, 1702 (Case 228; see note on Song 61).

95. *Poems on Several Occasions* . . . 1696. Set to music by J. Francis in *Mercurius Musicus*, 1699 (D. & M. 174). In the *Poems*, 1696, it is stated that the song is set by 'Mr. Akeroyde'.

WILLIAM WALSH (1663–1708)

96–8. *Letters and Poems. Amorous and Gallant* . . . 1692 (Hayward 136). Walsh was a man of fashion, 'ostentatiously splendid in his dress', and a Member of Parliament. He declared that there was not one folly that he had not committed in his devotion to women, with the exception of marriage. Song 98 was reprinted in *The Theatre of Ingenuity*, 1704 (Case 234).

ANONYMOUS

99. *Mercurius Musicus: or, The Monthly Collection of New Teaching Songs* . . . 1699 (D. & M. 174). Set to music by John Eccles. In this original printing only the first two stanzas occur. The third was added in *The Hive*, vol. iii, third edition, 1729 (Case 331 (3) *c*), and also reprinted in *The Cupid*, 1736 (Case 404). I have included it as the song seems hardly complete without it.

GEORGE FARQUHAR (1678–1707)

100. *Love and a Bottle* . . . 1699. Sung in Act III by Leanthe, disguised as a page. It is described as 'set by Mr. Richardson', but I have not traced the setting.

WILLIAM CONGREVE (1670–1729)

101. *The Way of the World* . . . 1700. Sung in Act III, Scene xii. 'Set by Mr. John Eccles', but I cannot trace the setting.

102. *Deliciae Musicae* . . . 1695 (D. & M. 131). Set by Henry Purcell. Also in *Thesaurus Musicus*, Book IV, 1695 (D. & M. 140), and *Orpheus Britannicus*, Book II, 1702 (D. & M. 200). The song was reprinted, with 'Celinda' altered to 'Selinda', in *Poetical Miscellanies*, Part V, 1704 (Case 172 (5) *a*), and in the third volume of Congreve's *Works*, 1710. Celinda is assumed to have been Mrs. Bracegirdle.

103. *Poetical Miscellanies: The Fifth Part*... 1704 (Case 172 (5) *a*). Reprinted in the third volume of Congreve's *Works*, 1710.

104. *The Third Volume of the Works of Mr. William Congreve; Containing Poems upon Several Occasions* . . . 1710.

ELIJAH FENTON (1683–1730)

105. *Oxford and Cambridge Miscellany Poems* . . . [1708] (Case 248). This miscellany was edited by Fenton, whose only claim to fame is that he assisted Pope in his translation of the *Odyssey*. He was a corpulent man who liked, as a woman who waited on him said, to 'lie a-bed and be fed with a spoon'. Lord Orrery, who was his pupil, said, 'he died of a great chair and two bottles of port a day'.

THE REV. THOMAS YALDEN (1670–1736)

106. *A New Collection of Poems on Several Occasions* [edited by Charles Gildon] . . . 1701. Reprinted in *Oxford and Cambridge Miscellany Poems* [1708] (Case 248) and in *The Theatre of Ingenuity*, 1704 (Case 234). This song was until recently attributed to Prior. Yalden was a friend of Addison and Congreve. Dr. Johnson said that 'his faults seem rather the omissions of idleness than the negligences of enthusiasm'.

SIR JOHN VANBRUGH (1664–1726)

107. *The Provok'd Wife* . . . 1697. Sung by Pipe in Act I.

MATTHEW PRIOR (1664–1721)

108, 109. *Poems on Several Occasions*... 1709. Both songs were also included in the folio edition of 1718, with minor textual alterations.

THOMAS OTWAY (1652–85)

110, 111. *The Works of . . . The Earls of Rochester and Roscommon . . . To which is added A Collection of Miscellany Poems. By the most Eminent Hands* . . . 1709 (Case 242*c*). J. C. Ghosh, on page 64 of the first volume of his edition of Otway's *Works*, 1932, refutes the claims of earlier editors that these two poems are by Otway. There is no evidence, however, that Mr. Ghosh had seen *The Works of Rochester and Roscommon*, 1709, where there is a clear attribution of both poems to Otway. Ault, the most careful of editors, gave Otway the credit for Song 110; so does *The Oxford Book of English Verse*.

JOHN SMITH (*fl.* 1713)

112, 113. *Poems upon Several Occasions. By Mr. Smith* . . . 1713. Hardly anything is known of this accomplished, if not notably original, poet. In a preface to his substantial book of verses he 'desires the Reader to look back to that Distance of Time in which they were compos'd'. Song 112 is an adaptation of Carew's 'The Mistake'.

HENRY CAREY (? 1687–1743)

114, 115. *Poems on Several Occasions* . . . 1713. It was not until the 1729 edition of Carey's *Poems* that 'Sally in our Alley' was printed.

INDEX OF FIRST LINES

INDEX OF AUTHORS

PRINTED IN GREAT BRITAIN
AT THE
UNIVERSITY PRESS
OXFORD
BY CHARLES BATEY
PRINTER
TO THE UNIVERSITY